"*Mail Order Annie*...a little Pembroke Welsh Corgi who taught her owner many lessons about life and living with dogs, which are shared in this charming and cleverly-organized book. Life with Annie, told lovingly in wonderful stories, inspired sensible and helpful lessons for raising any puppy. This delightful volume will be recommended as a 'must-read' for all my friends and new puppy-owners!"

> — *Lois E. Kay,*
> *Breeder of Champion Corgis &*
> *Past Board Member, Pembroke*
> *Welsh Corgi Club of the*
> *Potomac*

"**PUPPY KISSES ARE GOOD FOR THE SOUL** reaffirms the journey of joy, love, frustration and memories created through pet ownership. It is full of humor, typical owner angst and... the love between pets and humans. Through Howard's open way of sharing his memories, I relived numerous memories of my own pets — and also of the many animals I have treated over the years. He incorporates both the development of his relationship with Annie and the important basics of owner responsibility. Reading this book is a must for future pet-owners, as well as a genuine pleasure for owners current and past. Thank you, Annie, for giving Howard this wonderful story to write about."

> — *David Tayman, DVM*
> *(Chosen "One of Baltimore's*
> *Best Vets" by Baltimore*
> *Magazine)*

Puppy Kisses are *Good* for the *Soul*

& Other Important Lessons You & Your Dog Can Teach Each Other

Howard Weinstein & Mail Order Annie

Toad Hall Press & Puppy Paws Press

Puppy Kisses Are Good
For the Soul
&
Other Important Things
You & Your Dog Can Teach Each Other

Copyright © 2001 by Howard Weinstein

Cover and book design by Victoria Mark

Cover Photo by Howard Weinstein.
All interior photos Copyright © 2001 by Howard Weinstein,
except: Annie & Kimberly photo Copyright © 2001 by Marc Weinstein;
and Annie & Katie photo Copyright © 2001 by Deborah Greenberger.
Both photos reproduced with permission.

First printing: July 2001

ISBN: 1-893407-06-3

Toad Hall Press - Puppy Paws Press
RR2 - Box 2090
Laceyville, PA 18623
(570) 869-2942
Fax: (570) 869-1031
e-mail: ToadHallco@aol.com
Web site: www.laceyville.com/Toad-Hall

With thanks
to
Dr. David Tayman:
for his faith & trust

In memory
of
Vera Case:
a free spirit, gone too soon .

For
Mail Order Annie:
a little dog with the biggest heart —
the Spirit who guides me

Contents

Book One:

"The Amazing Life & Times of Mail Order Annie"

Book Two:
"Teach Your Puppy Well"
Puppy Prep 101

Puppy School 202

Introduction

It says on the cover "TWO BOOKS IN ONE!" Is it really?

Yes, it is. I was going to write two separate books. But then I thought, "Y'know what? *All this stuff* is important. What if people only buy one book, or the other? They're not going to get all the information they need. So why make people buy two books? Why not just make it a two-for-one deal?" So I did.

Two decades ago, a little furry football-sized puppy named Mail Order Annie changed my life. (That's her on the cover.) Sharing my daily existence with this little dog for 15 years, much to my surprise, made me a better human.

Because of Annie, I evolved into a dog trainer. Her spirit still guides me every day.

When I started my own training service, I decided to call it **DAY-ONE DOG TRAINING.** Why? Because the day they come to live with us is the best time to start teaching our puppies or dogs what *is* okay and what *isn't*. **Day-one.**

Many well-meaning people get dogs without realizing this. Since you're curious enough to be holding this book in your hand, here's the *truth*, right up front: training a puppy to be a civilized companion does not happen overnight. It takes *time*—a good two years. And it takes *commitment*—you have to be willing to put in some real effort. You owe it to yourself, and to your innocent puppy.

If you do the work, you'll reap the rewards. But if you don't, having a dog will not be the pleasure it should be. In fact, it may end up a disaster.

I want you to succeed. I want you to enjoy every day of your dog's life. If you read this book, follow the guidelines, teach your puppy with patience and love, and practice as often as you can, *you will succeed.*

There are lots of books on how to teach pups the basics of good behavior, some better than others. Methods vary widely, from harsh to gentle. Seems like there are as many opinions about dog training as there are trainers.

The more I've helped other people with their puppies and dogs, the more I concluded that there's a flaw in most of those books—as in many other kinds of "how-to" books: *they make things appear too easy*. The experts who write the books never seem to make any mistakes. Or, they don't admit they do. Meanwhile, we who are trying to learn their lessons make one mistake after another. Take me, for instance.

When I was nine, I badgered my parents into adopting a shelter puppy. After a week, it became obvious *nobody* in our family had a clue about raising a puppy. So I surrendered. The puppy went back to the shelter. And I've never forgotten that feeling of failure.

Twenty years later, grown up and living on my own, I tried again. After two weeks of chaos and frustration, I almost surrendered all over again. And I'll never forget how it felt to face that moment of truth for a second time.

This time, however, I mustered all my determination to make it work, to succeed at housebreaking my ten-pound Welsh Corgi puppy. Had I given up, I would have missed sharing 15 years of pure joy with my furry little miracle.

This book recounts many of my boneheaded blunders as I stumbled through the process of learning how to raise a puppy. Reading about my screw-ups may help you avoid the same ones. (But don't expect to be perfect; you'll probably make up some new mistakes of your very own!)

Navigating through puppyhood is challenging, even if you've done it before. If you *haven't* done it before—or did it so long ago you barely remember—there will be times when it seems near-impossible. But if I could do it, so can you.

So, telling you about all my mistakes is the first thing that makes this book different.

Here's the *second* difference—and the main reason I wrote this book. I wanted not only to pass along simple, common-sense training techniques that almost anyone should be able to master; I also wanted to give current and would-be dog owners an idea of what it's like to live with a wonderful, well-behaved dog for her entire lifetime.

And that, I believe, is something few (if any) training books have done before.

So I wrote the book I wish someone had given to me when I first got Annie. Then I would have had a blueprint of what to expect from sharing my life with a great dog. I would have fretted less and enjoyed more, especially in those first three formative years—when Annie was teaching me as much as I was training her.

With this book to guide me, I would not have been so tempted to give up on Annie when I grew weary of cleaning up puppy-potty accidents all over the apartment. I would have had a much better idea not only of the work involved, but of the rewards that waited just around the bend.

This book will tell you what I know now, but didn't know then: had I given up and hauled Annie back to her breeder, I would never have known the countless pleasures of having a dog. I would never have learned how to understand and teach dogs—while my *dogs* were teaching me to be a better person. I would never have set out to help other folks get the most out of having their own dogs.

Had I given up on Annie, my life would have been infinitely poorer.

So: *TWO BOOKS IN ONE?* Yes. One is filled with easy-to-use basic training lessons for you and your pup to work on as a team.

The other is the story of my life with Annie. Together, *both* books will help you understand and communicate with your dog. They'll help you build the best possible relationship with your pup, forging a new link in a chain unique in human history: the bond between us and our dogs.

To make the book user-friendly, the **Contents** pages clearly tell you what's where. You can read it in order. You can start with training lessons. You can start with Annie's story. Or you can skip around.

Whatever path you choose, if you *have* a dog, *want* a dog, or simply *love* dogs, there's something here for you.

In our 15 years together, my little Welsh Corgi pal taught me more about dogs than I ever knew there was to learn. Annie taught me how smart and determined dogs could be. How playful. And joyful. How sensitive. And kind. And, let's not forget, how forgiving of slights small and large. There's a bumper sticker, "To err is human—to forgive, canine." It's true.

From Annie, I learned to appreciate the fact that nobody greets you like your dog does. I learned that dogs, by nature and heart, are often the best of what we humans aspire to be. And, most unexpected of all, Annie taught me that a dog, well-loved and loving, can miraculously bring out the best in us.

No two dogs are exactly alike. But I suspect *all* good dogs share common traits. And living with them gives fortunate dog-owners mutual experiences, feelings and memories.

By writing about one very special dog and my years with her, I hope I've captured the universal joy dogs can bring to all our lives.

So, yes, this book is for people who've already had dogs. I hope you'll see something of your dog in mine.

But it's also for would-be and beginning dog-owners. I think I can help you get a successful start on this great adventure.

And it's for anyone who simply loves dogs. I hope you enjoy reading about Annie's lessons in love as much I've enjoyed learning them.

Open your home to a dog—and your dog will open your heart, soul and spirit in ways you've never even imagined. That's what Annie did for me. In doing so, she made me believe in miracles.

I hope this book helps you discover your own furry little miracle.

Annie taught me...

Puppy kisses are
good for the soul.

Annie's "TOP 10" Puppy-Raising Rules

1. Start teaching your dog or puppy the day you bring him home. *Don't delay!*

2. If there are things you *don't* want your puppy to do (for example: jumping, nipping, chewing the furniture, peeing on the rug), then *don't* let him do those things!

3. If there are things you *do* want your puppy to do, then start *teaching* her those things right away!

4. Puppies need to earn freedom, by virtue of behavior, training and maturity. Until he's trained and "grown-up," *no* puppy should be given unsupervised free run of your home.

5. The single *best way* to manage your puppy's behavior, stop him from doing negative things, and get him to do positive things is to *use a leash*—even in the house!

6. Puppies are a lot like two-year-old children: given the opportunity, they're very good at getting into very bad trouble—and they can do it instantly. So they need to be supervised by a responsible adult or older child constantly.

7. When you can't supervise your puppy, make sure he's safe in his crate, or in a puppy-proofed exercise pen.

8. It's much easier to teach *good* habits than it is to break *bad* ones.

9. Don't give commands you can't enforce. Every time you do—and your pup doesn't comply—you're teaching her she doesn't have to listen… which is the exact opposite of what you're trying to teach her.

10. *Make training fun*, for both you and your puppy. Expect progress, not perfection. If training sessions are fun, your puppy will become an eager student.

Moses may have stopped at ten commandments, but Annie has a few extras for you:

11. Teach yourself to be *firm but gentle*. Puppies need structure; the more they understand about what's expected of them, the better behaved they will be.

12. Teach your pup to love his crate. Start this the very first day. The sooner you succeed, the happier you and your puppy will both be.

13. Don't be afraid to reward your pup with praise, affection and occasional treats. The only way he knows when he's doing something right is when you tell him.

All of these "commandments" are discussed in greater detail throughout this book—some in more than one place and context. When it comes to good advice, a little redundancy never hurts!

Book One

"The Amazing
Life & Times
of
Mail Order
Annie"

Part One
EARLY DAYS

First Failures...

But for a random twist of fate, I would never have known Mail Order Annie. I would not have ventured out on strange roads, metal dog crate stowed in the rear of my hatchback Dodge Omni, bound for a pastoral corner of northern New Jersey to which I'd never been before and to which I haven't returned since.

I'd always wanted a dog. I grew up in the 1960s, when dogs were the traditional pet of choice for suburban families. Cats were around, here and there. But most moms still stayed home, so it was okay to have a pet that needed to be looked after and walked during the day. There's no question many people today find cats more suited to busy lifestyles that now keep many of us out of our homes from dawn to well past dark. I'm convinced that's the reason cats have apparently passed dogs in numerical popularity in recent years.

Dogs do require more commitment. Cats offer the luxury of being pets of convenience.

But when it's 1964, and you're not quite ten, and your friends have dogs, and you love to pet them and play with them and volunteer to walk them (the dogs, not the friends), you're more than willing to step up and make that commitment, if that's what it takes to convince your parents to let you get a dog.

Even if you have only the haziest notion of the definition of "commitment."

And even less notion of the specifics of dog care.

Understatement: We were *not* dog people. My Aunt Naomi and Uncle Jack in Queens, New York had an old graying standard Poodle named

Patsy. She was the only dog in our entire extended family of uncles, aunts and cousins. I liked Patsy. My mother did not. My parents hadn't had dogs as kids, and in all likelihood hadn't known many. Pet dogs were probably uncommon in walk-up Bronx tenements during the Depression. So the fact is, my parents were essentially indifferent to dogs.

And I faced another obstacle. *Gesundheit.*

My father was allergic to dogs. This wasn't just an easy excuse offering my parents refuge from a child quite unwilling to take "no" for a final answer. Dad really *was* allergic—red-eyed, nose-blowing, house-shaking-sneeze allergic.

To this day, I don't know how I convinced my parents to allow a puppy to enter our home with the intent of sticking around for ten or fifteen years. I wheedled. Cajoled. Whined.

Promised to do whatever. I may have made some sacred vows we've all mercifully forgotten.

Whatever I did; it worked. Mom caved. We made plans to visit the Bide-a-Wee Animal Shelter near our Long Island, New York home to find a puppy. The adoption fee would be ten dollars. I would have to earn it. So I went to work.

Literally.

I spent the summer of '64 sweeping neighbors' garages, cleaning up basements, and doing whatever other odd jobs a nine-year-old could do to earn fifty cents or a couple of bucks. Late that season, I had the cash. More excited than I'd ever been in my life, I willed Mom's old Ford down the road to the animal shelter.

We picked out a six-week-old mixed breed, part Beagle, part Basset Hound. We named her Cookie, though I have no idea why. I haven't bothered to say she was adorable. She was a puppy. All puppies are adorable. Lucky for them.

Cookie was tan and white with floppy ears. She cried on the short drive home. I did my best to comfort her. When we got back to the house, she fell asleep. At the time, none of us knew that's pretty much what six-week-old puppies do. Cry, play, poop, eat and sleep.

Cookie spent her first night as my dog in my room. Notice I didn't use the word *sleep* in that sentence. That's the one thing she didn't

Here I am at 9, holding Cookie, my Beagle/Bassett puppy for a week

do. She yipped, cried, yowled, peed, pooped and generally made us wonder if getting a puppy was really such a swell idea.

By the next night, Cookie had been banished to the basement. We had one of those above-ground backyard pools, the kind with the wire mesh frame to give it shape, and a vinyl liner to hold the water. We took the three-foot-high wire frame and used it to form a round basement pen for our puppy. We spread newspapers, gave her water and a bed.

And prayed she would sleep.

She did. And the next morning, when we opened the basement door, there was tiny little Cookie waiting at the top of the basement stairs. With very little apparent trouble or effort, she'd managed to scale the walls of her prison. And with considerable courage in her puppy heart, she learned how to climb a full flight of steep stairs.

I wish I could tell you Cookie had a long and happy life with our family. I'm sure she had a long and happy life with somebody. But it wasn't us. After a week of my father's sneezing, and the rest of us pretty much clueless about how to deal with this furry little dynamo, I surrendered.

Tearfully, we took Cookie back to the shelter. I felt like a failure. For all I know, those feelings of inadequacy have haunted me for life.

And a day later, with no announcement, my mother secretly drove back to the shelter all by herself to retrieve Cookie. Of all people, Mom had fallen in love with that little dog and wanted to take her back for a second chance. But someone else had already been captivated by those floppy ears and brown eyes, and by that time Cookie was pooping in someone else's house. We never saw her again. I hope she made another family happy.

My family made what I think is the most common mistake among new dog owners: We were totally unprepared. In fact, we were *so* unprepared, we didn't even *know* how much we didn't know. Now, as a professional trainer all these years later, I see similarly unprepared folks all the time. The common refrain: "I had *no idea…*"

Sad Truth

- ☙ As many as half of all dog adoptions and purchases end in failure

- ☙ Various sources estimate that animal shelters euthanize between 2 and 5 million dogs each year.

- ☙ Almost half of all dogs surrendered to animal shelters were owned less than one year!

- ☙ An incredible 96% of dogs that end up in shelters were never obedience-trained—which is usually why they get dumped by exasperated owners

(Sources: American Animal Hospital Association and American Veterinary Medical Association)

In Cookie's case, we also didn't know that six-week-old puppies don't really belong in my house or yours. They belong with their mothers and brothers and sisters. They're still learning how to be dogs. Now I know that puppies should be at least seven or eight weeks old before leaving the nest, even a week or two older if you want to have a fighting chance of housebreaking them quickly.

But back in the late summer of '64, I didn't know any of this. All I knew was, I'd wanted a dog *more than anything in the world.* I'd had one, for a week. And I'd probably blown my childhood chance of ever having one again.

Annie taught me...

If you're going to try something new, be prepared! Somebody out there already knows what we need to know. If we find and use that information, we can enhance our odds for success!

Second Chances

It took almost twenty years before my next chance to get a dog—and not before Mother Nature rolled her dice. One puppy was to die before another became my best friend.

In the Spring of 1981, I faced my twenty-seventh birthday. Cindi Casby, my on-again-off-again girlfriend of the previous four years, was about to graduate from college. We'd been having problems, but we decided that she would move into my Westbury, New York apartment when she got out of school. Not the best decision either of us have ever made, for a lot of reasons that have nothing much to do with this book.

Fortunately, it was a two-bedroom apartment. My first roommate had recently vacated his half to go to law school. So Cindi would have her own room.

About the only thing we agreed on over those first couple of months was that we would get two dogs. His and hers. Cindi had her heart set on a Collie.

I *thought* I wanted a Basset Hound—until we went to a dog show to chat with some breeders, and I met a fifty-five pound Basset (aptly named

Miss Piggy).

Our apartment was not that big. With Cindi getting a Collie, it made sense for me to get something smaller. The problem was, I had no back-up breeds in mind. So I did some reading. I didn't want a really tiny dog. Whatever I chose, it would have to be a big dog in a little package to hold its own with a male Collie.

That's when I stumbled onto one of the best-kept secrets of the dog world: the Pembroke Welsh Corgi.

Corgis never seem to rise above mid-rank on the annual breed-popularity lists. I didn't know any Corgis. I'd never even seen one in real life. But I learned they were rugged little dogs with enough heart and soul to herd goats, sheep, even cows. The official American Kennel Club Standard described them this way: "Low-set, strong, sturdily built and active, giving an impression of substance and stamina in a small space... Outlook bold, but kindly. Expression intelligent and interested."

That sounded like the dog for me. So I found a breeder named Yvonne Sileo. She happened to live not far from where I worked in Huntington, Long Island, and I visited her during one lunch hour. Mrs. Sileo took me into her big yard, where she had a bunch of Corgis in several kennel runs. They all rushed eagerly to the fronts of their pens. They jockeyed for position, all standing on their hind legs, little round front paws braced against the fence wire. Every bright-eyed Corgi face smiled at me. And every little pink tongue tried to lick my hands. They were enchanting. And I fell in love with Corgis.

The breeder had a litter due at just the right time for me to get my Corgi pup at the same time as Cindi would get her Collie. We wanted our puppies to be best pals and wanted them to arrive on the same day, so neither one would be able to pull rank by virtue of who got there first. By early August, Cindi and I would have our dogs.

When my litter was born, there were problems. First, there were only two puppies instead of the usual half-dozen or more. One died almost immediately. And the mother showed no interest in nursing the sole survivor.

So Mrs. Sileo took him out and hand-raised him, telling me there were positives and negatives to raising a puppy this way. He'd certainly be a people-oriented dog. He was also likely to be spoiled rotten.

I met my puppy when he was five weeks old. He was a tri-color, mostly black with tan and white markings. And little tan "eyebrows." Even at five weeks, he seemed fearless. I thought long and hard about a name. And failed to come up with anything remotely proper yet original.

We went back to see him again at seven weeks. By then, his characteristic Corgi bat-ears had developed enough strength to stand up. Those giant ears swiveled independently as he homed in on all the sounds in a world still quite new to him. Like radar dishes. And that's when we came up with a name: *Radar*. Since we were fans of the *M*A*S*H** television series, Cindi decided to name her Collie Hawkeye.

We had names. We bought leashes, collars, dishes and toys. All we needed were the pups.

Two weeks before we were to bring Radar and Hawkeye home, I went away for the weekend. When I returned from my trip, Cindi told me Radar's breeder had called with bad news. A predatory new disease called parvovirus had been striking terror into the hearts of breeders and pet owners alike that year. Somehow, Radar had become infected with parvo. Despite Mrs. Sileo's best efforts, my puppy-to-be had died over the weekend.

I was stunned. Beyond that, I wasn't sure what I felt. I mean, Radar hadn't really been *my* dog yet. I'd only seen him twice. Only spent an hour or two with him. I didn't know him, and he didn't really know me.

Aside from confused feelings, I had a more pressing problem: in order for our simultaneous-puppy-arrival plan to work, I had to locate another Corgi pup of the right age in less than two weeks.

Using a list from the Pembroke Welsh Corgi Club of America, I called almost every Corgi breeder in Connecticut, New York and New Jersey over the next few days. Nobody had what I needed. But they were all sympathetic and helpful, and several directed me to other breeders they knew who weren't on the current Corgi Club list.

I was almost out of options when I found Hillendale Kennel in Lebanon, New Jersey. The breeder's name was Terry Galbraith, and she happened to have a litter that was exactly the right age. She had three puppies still not spoken for, two boys and a girl. I made a date to come up to her house.

But the situation wasn't ideal. Before you actually choose a puppy to take home with you, all the books advise prospective dog owners to meet the breeder; meet the doggie father and mother if at all possible, to size up physical and temperamental characteristics; and, of course, meet the puppies.

But because of our arbitrary goal of my getting a puppy at the same time as Cindi got her fluffball Hawkeye, I'd be tossing the crate in the car and making the two-hour drive with the intention of coming home with a puppy I'd only just met. I began to have doubts about the whole project.

And I wrestled with those doubts the whole way up.

A word about New Jersey. When most people think of New Jersey, they think "New Jersey Turnpike." Or Newark. Or the smokestacked skyline of the north-central Jersey territories fouling the air adjacent to New York City. Scenic images do not blossom in the mind's eye.

In fairness, much of New Jersey is beautiful rolling farms and deep green woodlands. Small towns with tree-lined Main Streets instead of industrial fortresses fogged under a polluted haze.

As I remember it, Hillendale Kennel turned out to be just outside one of those picturesque towns with small shops and stone walls. I felt a little better as I drove up the gravel lane and parked outside the breeder's house. Plenty of grass and trees all around. Even a small pond. Not a smokestack in sight.

Mrs. Galbraith brought me into her kitchen to meet the three remaining puppies. They were nine weeks old. Little furry footballs with silky ears, needle-sharp teeth and bright brown eyes. I sat on the floor with them and tried to remember all the puppy-choosing tips I'd read.

Because I'd been set to get a male puppy until Radar's untimely demise, I looked initially at the Hillendale boys. When I called the first one, trying to get his attention by sweet talk and hand-claps, he went the other way. I could not get that dog to come to me. Not critical, perhaps, not at this stage and in these circumstances. But not a recommendation either.

The other boy also had a one-track mind: scampering outside and playing in the dirt. I did not stand in his way.

The third puppy was the only female. Her coat was the classic Corgi "red and white"—actually a rich auburn-tan, with white markings on her paws, face, chest and belly. Her mighty ears had not yet stood up. And unlike her brothers, she seemed quite interested in meeting me. She marched up, all purposeful directness and curiosity, and began licking my hand.

She let me pick her up and set her gently down on her back. She wasn't thrilled about the position. But she didn't kick and bite the way some puppies will. She simply accepted it as an occasionally necessary chore in life, letting a person up-end her like this. I got what I needed out of that textbook maneuver: the knowledge that she was neither fearful nor aggressively dominant.

I let her up. And we played. Her attention never wavered. After nearly an hour of this, I heard a soft *whummp* behind me. A large cat, previously sunning itself on a wide windowsill, had jumped to the floor with considerable authority. As the cat stretched, the male pups skittered and scattered to the safe corners of the kitchen.

The little female held her ground, squared her shoulders in challenge to the cat easily half again her size, and summoned several brave puppy barks. The cat absorbed this impertinent show of disrespect, and sauntered off in a huff.

I was smitten. In my hour with her, the little red-and-white female had shown me everything I needed to know about her. I paid for her. And we drove home.

This time, the name came easily. In the short interval since I'd named and lost poor little Radar, another loss had shaken my life. Folksinger and social activist Harry Chapin had been killed in an auto accident on the Long Island Expressway less than three weeks before I picked out my New Jersey puppy. Best known for his story-songs *"Taxi"* and *"Cats in the Cradle,"* Harry had been a Long Island resident. I'd been a big fan of his music, enjoyed many of his concerts, and been inspired by his selfless devotion to such diverse causes as alleviating world hunger and supporting the arts.

One of my favorite Harry Chapin songs was a sweet 1973 ballad about a North Dakota farmer arriving at a prairie railroad depot to meet his mail-order bride. Even all these years later, I never tire of hearing the song, and it always brings a lump to my throat. It wasn't one of Harry's radio-hits, but I think it was one of his very best. And, judging by the heartfelt way he sang it in concert, of all the songs he wrote in his too-short life, I've always believed it must have been one of his favorites, too.

10-week-old Annie, one ear up and one down

It's called *"Mail Order Annie."*

And that's what I named my puppy. I sang her the song on our way home.

Bathroom "Boot Camp"

Considering that Cindi and I didn't quite know what we were doing in getting two puppies at the same time, things worked out pretty well. Lucky for us!

Annie and Hawkeye went directly from playing with their littermates to playing with each other. They bonded instantly. And they became best friends.

But they almost didn't have the chance. My relationship with Annie nearly foundered on the shoals of housebreaking.

Nine weeks old when I brought her home, Annie was fairly reliably paper-trained. Hawkeye was a month older, and fairly reliably housebroken. Paper training, of course, is the questionable practice of teaching your puppy to relieve itself on newspapers spread on the floor. *Indoors.*

Housebreaking, on the other hand, teaches the dog to go exclusively *outdoors.*

You'll notice I used the words *fairly reliably* to describe both puppies. That's because very few puppies master immediately and perfectly the art of bathroom etiquette. The idea is to make sure they grasp the concept as quickly as possible, and forgive the inevitable mistakes that will occur until they're old enough to control their bodily functions (and then some). Some pups need a grace period of months, some need weeks, and other canine superstars need only days. Of course, some never learn, but that's usually because of the people, not the dog. I was a case in point.

I actually took a two-week "paternity leave" to stay home and take care of the puppies. We hoped that would be enough for them to learn proper potty training. After that, while we were at work, they'd spend their days gated in our kitchen, with a floor liberally covered by newspapers to catch mistakes.

Building on what he'd learned at his breeder's, Hawkeye was a quick study. But Annie just didn't seem to be catching on.

Of course, the fault was mine, not hers. I committed the cardinal potty-training sin of having her sometimes go indoors, (theoretically) on paper, and sometimes outdoors. It wasn't working. And I was getting very tired of cleaning up indoor messes. I seriously considered bringing her back to her breeder and giving up on the idea of having my own dog.

Then I read our books again, and realized *my* inconsistency was confusing the hell out of her. I was trying to take the lazy way out, opting for the supposed convenience of paper-training, and taking her outside only when it suited me. She would have to be taught to go outdoors and *only* outdoors. And *soon.*

So Annie and I enrolled in bathroom boot-camp. For an entire weekend, I followed housebreaking instructions to the letter. My every waking

Not So Loud, But Very Clear

Almost all puppy-owners get frustrated with their babies at one time or another. And most of us are guilty of losing our tempers, or even yelling at our pups.

- ❧ If you've got to yell, keep it short. Use the curse of the day to blow off steam, yes. But beware of lengthy and loud tirades.

- ❧ The only thing yelling accomplishes is to teach your puppy to be afraid of you. Yelling doesn't teach him anything positive.

- ❧ And it doesn't deliver what we want: a housebroken dog.

moment revolved around her elimination needs. Out of nowhere, I'd have to develop an instinct for anticipating when she had to go. I'd have to get her outside before it was too late, give her the chance to poop or pee (or both), rain or shine, and then sing her praises. All to shape the desired behavior pattern. It was a daunting task, and I didn't think I could do it.

Fortunately, Annie never had a moment's doubt. As I was just learning, that was Annie's general take on herself and the world.

Once I figured out how to communicate to her what I wanted, it was as if she said to me: "Oh. Okay. I can do that. Why didn't you say so?"

In that single weekend, Annie housebroke herself (with slight assistance from me—it was my job to snap on her leash and open the doors for her). And for the rest of her life, she never again went to the bathroom inside unless she was sick and couldn't help it.

So we kept Annie. Lucky for me.

Annie taught me...

To teach almost anything (to a person or dog), we need to figure out how to communicate clearly, so our pupils will understand what we want. And then we need to be patient. Treat a student the way you'd like to be treated if you were trying to learn something.

Annie & Hawkeye

As it turned out, Annie and Hawkeye had personalities that meshed perfectly. And comically.

Hawkeye had the sweetest disposition I've ever seen in a dog. He was loving and trusting. Childlike and innocent. And fortunately not dominant.

It quickly became clear that Annie was, by nature, born to rule. As she grew older, she took every opportunity to broadcast the immutable fact that she was *the* Alpha female, with dominion over all she surveyed.

Even the Doberman Pinscher that lived upstairs.

When I first got Annie, we lived on the ground floor of a two-story garden apartment building. No one could enter or leave without passing our front door. For the year or so that the Doberman lived there, whenever Annie heard the *clikk-clikk* of doggie nails on the hardwood floor above us, she would race to our door. When the Doberman and her owner went past, Annie barked and growled from behind our closed door, just enough to make her point.

One day, we were heading out for our walk just as the Doberman came in from outdoors. The Doberman's head happened to be precisely outside our door at the moment I opened it. I didn't know who was outside. But *Annie* did. And the poor Doberman found herself facing snapping Corgi teeth. I've never seen a dog so startled. I yanked Annie back inside and slammed the door before the other dog could regain her senses and realize the dog

Puppies manage to sleep comfortably in the oddest positions.

attempting to intimidate her was probably smaller than some of her chew-toys.

Annie never let her diminutive physical stature get in her way. Yes, this attitude carried with it potential for trouble. Fortunately, she never came face-to-face with a dog willing and ready to challenge her. She'd speak first, and didn't bother to ask questions. And most other dogs accepted the world according to Annie.

It's possible living with Hawkeye fortified her natural inclinations. Even though Hawk grew to three times Annie's height and weight, he went along with her dominance. It's not because he was dumb. He later went on to win an impressive number of obedience trophies and ribbons. It just never seemed to occur to him that he didn't have to be subservient to a Welsh Corgi who regularly evoked laughter by walking *under* Hawkeye's belly, without even ducking her head to accommodate those outsized ears of hers.

I should make it clear that Annie was never vicious to other dogs. Not that there weren't times when I was afraid of what she might do to another animal. For years, when she'd growl and snap, I'd hold her leash tightly and pull her away from confrontation, as with that surprised Doberman.

Then, one time, with the cooperation of another dog owner, we decided to let nature take its somewhat-controlled course. With leashes held slack but firmly in hand, we let Annie and the other dog (a Shetland sheepdog) get close. Annie barked loudly, but not fearfully. Then she snapped her teeth at his nose. The other dog jerked his head back. And having laid down the law, Annie proceeded to ignore him. The pecking order was settled with very little fuss.

The more I learned about dog training and canine psychology, the more I realized Annie knew *exactly* what she was doing. She was in complete control. She had no intention of biting the other dog. She didn't need to. She simply used universal dog language to tell him who was boss. There's a clear line between dominance and aggression. Thankfully, Annie never crossed it.

After that, I never worried about her behavior again. I watched with interest and amusement as she used her proven techniques with amazing confidence on a variety of dogs, of both genders and various ages. It was especially amusing to see her deal later in life with puppies. By then, she plainly considered herself the Dowager Empress, deserving of proper respect from all her canine subjects.

Puppies would see a dog of her compact size and assume she was another puppy, eager to play. Annie would disabuse them of that idea with little wasted motion. And as they grew older, and far larger than she, these former puppies would continue to treat her with the respect she warranted, even though they'd keep asking her to play.

But Annie never had to enforce her dominance over her pal Hawkeye.

He never seriously challenged it. Although there was one time he objected rather strenuously. It was just one of those days when he didn't feel like playing, and Annie kept pestering him. He wanted simply to lie on the floor and be left alone. But Annie refused to give up.

Finally, when Hawkeye decided he'd taken one nip, poke or jump too many, he rose in a flash to his full-grown height. He *roared* out a single bark right in Annie's face. She *instantly* flipped over onto her back, her little arms and legs sticking straight up. She looked like an upended bug. It was the classic canine sign of submission—and the only time in her entire life I ever saw Annie in that position (other than to get a belly-rub). She had this startled look on her face that clearly said: "Hey, I thought *I* was in charge."

Quite a wing-span on those ears. Only a low center of gravity kept her from getting airborne on windy days.

Satisfied he'd made his point, Hawkeye saw no need to pursue the matter. He ambled off to take his nap. And he never did anything like that again.

I don't want to give the impression that Annie mistreated Hawkeye.

Quite the contrary. They truly enjoyed each other's company. For the entire three years they were together, they never had an actual fight. In fact, other than Hawkeye's one outburst, I can't recall them ever exchanging so much as another cross bark.

And Annie did make one on-going concession to companionship.

For some reason we never were able to figure out, Hawk liked to lick Annie's ears, inside and out. Every now and then, he'd just lie down next to her, and do it. And we never saw her object. Instead, she'd sit with this long-suffering look on her face and stay there until he stopped. Then she'd shake her head a few times, fluff up her dignity and walk away—with very wet ears.

Annie the Actress

I've often thought that folks planning to have kids should be required to have a dog first. Not that I'm equating the two. There are certainly differences. For one, you can leave a puppy home alone, either in her crate or in the kitchen behind a safety gate. Try the same thing with a baby, and you'll end up on the local evening news accused of child abuse. Plus, you don't have to pay for a dog to go to college, and they never ask for the car keys (although some have been known to *steal* the keys).

Still, for many young adults, single or married, having a puppy is their first introduction to the nerve-wracking notion of being *totally responsible* for another life. And dogs are much more needy creatures than tropical fish or even cats. By that I mean you have to see to their basic physical needs by walking and feeding them several times a day.

Dogs also have emotional needs. As pack animals, they need interaction with their human pack members. You have to play with them, train them and pay attention to them, to maximize their mental health and happiness.

One of my training clients summed up the experience neatly. Her boyfriend had given her an adorable and spirited beagle puppy for Christmas. The gift came as a complete surprise to her, and she was (you guessed it) *totally unprepared*. (*Never* surprise someone with a puppy!) After only two weeks, she confessed to me: "This is the most stressful thing I've ever done in my entire life!"

So, while having a dog isn't *exactly* like having a baby, it's a BIG STEP up on the responsibility scale—higher than washing your car, for instance.

Canine caretaking includes regular visits to the vet. In puppyhood, those visits may be fairly frequent, for various inoculations and lab tests.

This is the time of their lives when many puppies develop a fear of even setting foot in the vet's waiting room, much less going into an actual exam room and getting hoisted up onto a table.

Think about how you'd feel if every time you went to the doctor, somebody picked you up and put you on a small slippery platform, oh, say, *four or five stories above the floor*. And then this giant came along to pry open your jaws, poke your ears, and stick you with needles while another giant held you down. You probably wouldn't like it either.

To avoid such lifelong trauma, most vets and vet technicians try to be very gentle and reassuring—to both your pet and you. They stroke the animals before and after exams, and offer them treats. I can remember back to when I was little kid, and both doctors and barbers always gave out lollipops as peace offerings after they were done with me. Such tokens do help a little bit.

Annie never had a problem with vet visits. She marched right in like she owned the place. And she was pretty much fearless up on that exam table. Never in her entire life did she even attempt to bite a health professional.

But I'll never forget one of our early visits. She was in for her first heartworm test. After drawing some blood, the vet tied a piece of gauze around her arm to help the tiny needle-prick clot up. I put Annie down on the floor and we went out to the front desk to pay our bill. I held Annie's leash in one hand as I wrote a check with the other.

Then I looked down to find Annie hobbling around on three legs, her bandage flapping, looking like a little canine refugee from the famous "Spirit of '76" painting of battered Revolutionary War heroes on the march with fife and drum. All she needed was a little flag. She held her wounded arm high in the air, as if to announce to the world, "Hey! Look what they did to me!"

Annie taught me...

If you get mad at your puppy—and you will—take a moment to look at her face. You can't stay mad at a puppy face. They make us smile. When you smile, you relax. And so does your puppy. Perspective is restored. Life goes on.

Coffee-Table "Fortress of Solitude"

Whenever we gave Annie and Hawkeye new chew toys, we always felt we had to be fair and give an equivalent toy to each dog. Just like having two kids. Rawhide was the usual chew-fare. Sometimes chips, sometimes knotted "bones". Hawkeye would take his, happily plop down wherever he happened to be, and start chewing.

Annie would grab hers and scramble under the large hexagonal coffee table centered in our living room. The design of the table's legs and side supports made it the perfect fort for a Welsh Corgi. There was no way a Collie could squeeze under there. Annie knew her treasures were safe.

Hawkeye would blissfully gnaw on his rawhide, completely unaware that Annie had him under full-time surveillance as she chomped on hers. After a while, Hawkeye (who had a much shorter attention span than Annie) would drop his toy, perhaps to go into the kitchen for some water, or maybe just to see what else was going on.

The moment he'd amble off, Annie would slip out, grab his toy and scurry back into her stronghold. Then, inevitably, Hawk would come back to resume his chewing—and find his toy gone. He'd look at Annie, see that she had both—and then he'd whine for help, because there wasn't anything he could do about Corgi larceny.

Now, Hawkeye also had a preference for what we called "pre-chewed" rawhide. Despite his larger jaws, he'd chew his toys much more slowly than Annie. That meant the one she'd taken from him was still close to being new, and therefore a greater challenge to her. So Cindi or I would reach into Annie's fortress, take her original toy which she'd already softened, and give that one to Hawkeye. And he'd be happy again. Even happier, because he got a soft and slimy pre-chewed toy.

Annie's best pal Hawkeye: sweetest dog I ever knew

We always thought Annie was the leader of this toy-trade behavior. Now that I think of it, maybe it was Hawkeye who was the mastermind, knowing he'd get the toy he wanted in the end. If so, it was a great act.

Pillows & Puppydog Tails

Just to make matters confusing, there are two distinct kinds of Welsh Corgis. There's the Pembroke Welsh Corgi, and the Cardigan.

Both are named for shires (or counties) in Wales. The major difference is that Cardigans have tails and Pembrokes do not. Other than that, they look quite similar. Both are long and low, with foxy faces and tall pointed ears. Both were bred for herding animals.

Yet, according to dog historians, the two Corgi breeds are not from the same original stock. Over the years, apparently, crossbreeding resulted in making the Pembrokes and Cardigans look more and more alike.

Except for that obvious difference: the tail.

Pembrokes are either bred to have naturally bobbed tails, or their tails are docked when the infant pups are just a few days old.

There's a whole debate in the dog world over tail docking and ear cropping. Some dog-lovers insist any such "alterations" are nothing short of barbaric mutilation, and should be stopped. Others think the argument is a lot of fuss over nothing. I'm steering clear of the entire conflict.

But now that I've owned and been around Pembroke Corgis for the better part of two decades, a dog without a tail seems perfectly normal to me. In fact, I sometimes look at a dog *with* a tail and think, "Isn't *that* peculiar!"

For other people, it's quite the opposite. The funniest thing is when people who've known a Corgi for quite some time suddenly open their eyes wide and exclaim: "Hey! Your dog doesn't have a tail!"

I'm sure I'm not the only Corgi owner tempted to respond with: "*Ohmygod*!! It must've fallen off! Help me find it!" But that wouldn't be kind. And Corgis are generally kind. So should their owners be.

It's true that dog tails are wonderfully expressive things. They wag furiously. They stiffen at alert. They hang low. Tails speak plainly. Yet, as far as I knew, Annie never missed her tail (if she'd ever had one). In lieu of a tail, her entire rear end would wiggle back and forth when she was happy.

For Annie, Hawk's having a tail was far more important than not having one of her

Annie on her favorite pillow: Hawkeye's tail

24

own. Collies, of course, have glorious furry flags for tails. Sometimes Hawkeye's tail served Annie as a toy or a playmate. But we had no doubt that Annie loved that tail most of all when the dogs would lie down for a rest. Hawkeye would stretch out on his side or belly. Once he got comfortable, Annie would circle to his rear, find the right spot—and use his tail as her pillow. She would snuggle close to him, and bury her face in his fur. They'd fall asleep that way, and never looked more tranquil.

Say "Cheese"

When you get a puppy, you may be so busy trying to take care of your new baby that it's easy to forget something very simple: *taking pictures*!

My one regret about having Annie is that I only snapped a handful of photos during her first few weeks.

I have just one blurry picture of her with both ears down. And just a single picture with one ear up and one down. I cherish those few that I do have, and wish I'd taken more.

Best Bet: have a loaded point-and-shoot camera handy at all times. You never know when your pup is going to present you with fleeting, impossibly cute moments. Don't be one of those dog owners always exclaiming: "Darn! If only I had my camera!"

Continue taking pictures as your pal grows up.

They're not adorable little pups for long. But they'll always be beautiful, so document your dog's life. You'll be glad you did.

Annie taught me...

Life goes by too fast. I've never been sorry about photos I did take of people, places and pets. But there are lots of photos I'm sorry I didn't take.

Doors & Gates I

Annie did not like doors. Or gates. To be more accurate, she didn't like anything that kept her from going wherever she darn-well pleased. Or stopped her from seeing what was on the other side.

If I'd close a door as I went into another room, Annie would soon be pushing at it with her nose. If the door didn't give way, she'd scratch gently with her little hand.

Umm...her *hand?* Yes, I know dogs technically have paws and legs, not hands and arms. But to see Annie use her front paws, well, you'd have to conclude, "Nope, those're hands all right." Corgis have stout front legs and adorable, round forepaws. When a Corgi lies down on her belly, her arms...umm, front legs...barely extend to the tip of her nose. This puts those front paws in the perfect position for holding things to be chewed upon, without any of the awkwardness of dogs with longer limbs that must be folded somehow to be useful as hands.

So, yes, *Annie had hands.*

But we were talking about doors and gates. I think part of her reaction was guided by the natural canine instinct to know everything possible about her immediate environment. Annie just liked to know where people and things were at all times.

The gate we made to keep both dogs in the kitchen when they were young was the obstruction she hated the most. Like virtually all puppies, these two chewed on unauthorized items from time to time. This included a surplus kitchen chair, baseboard moldings, even the walls. We figured if we kept them in the kitchen when we weren't there to supervise them, at least we'd limit the damage to one room.

Our gate consisted of an old-fashioned wooden accordion-type child gate, pulled out to the proper size, and firmly attached to a home-made wood frame. We put the latch near the top, so we could reach it easily whether going in or out of the kitchen. Defeating that gate became one of Annie's

Making the best of a bad situation:
Annie uses her nemesis as a chin-rest.
Note the seriously-chewed wood to the left of her nose.

26

primary occupations for the first three years of her life.

And yet, the gate also ended up challenging her creativity and honing her intelligence. It became jailer, playmate and even stage for our ever-inventive Annie.

Her first assaults were frontal and primal: she tried *chewing* her way through. And she certainly made her marks on the slats and frame. We in turn tried to discourage this, since we didn't want her ingesting chunks of wood. We tried some Bitter Apple, the venerable, unpleasant-tasting liquid most pets find pretty objectionable. It's been in use for decades and it generally does the job. Spray it on items that outlaw teeth find irresistible, and it often breaks the habit before it gets established.

Bitter Apple worked in the short term. But the tart-tasting liquid contains a lot of alcohol, and it dries and evaporates fairly quickly. So Annie would chew some more.

Then we escalated this battle of the wills: we resorted to Tabasco sauce. Even to human tastebuds, Tabasco packs quite a wallop. To dogs, with their super-sensitive noses (and remember, smell and taste are closely related senses), it must be the equivalent of ten-alarm chili. But we were desperate.

So we slathered the stuff on all the gate parts she would habitually attack. The hot sauce worked. Annie stopped chewing. And resorted to acting.

She'd squeeze her head through the bars and rest it there, looking for all the world like a colonial criminal in the stocks. I'm sure she was hoping for sympathy. Instead, she got laughs.

Unable to find a way *through* the gate, she then used it for her amusement. Our living room had a hardwood floor, which was a little higher than the tile floor of the kitchen. The way we mounted the accursed gate left about an inch between the horizontal bottom of the gate frame and the molding that edged the hardwood floor.

This formed a natural trough. To complete the playing field, we had an area rug in the living room. Between the rug and the kitchen gate were two feet of open hardwood floor. And this is where Annie invented her own little game.

Stuck in the kitchen, she would pick up her blue rubber ball in her mouth, stick her head through the gate, and drop the ball into that trough formed by the hardwood edging and the bottom of the gate. Then she'd lie on her belly and slip her hands under the gate. And she would intentionally *poke* the ball out of the trough, up onto the hardwood floor. It would roll, hit the edge of the area rug, and roll *back* into the trough at the gate. And Annie would hit it again. And again. And again. *Voila—Corgi Punchball.*

Annie taught me...

It's easier to teach good habits
than it is to break bad ones.

Gourmet Wallboard

IDEALLY: Puppies chew only on authorized toys that help them cut their
new teeth, burn off some of that endless supply of energy, and keep them
from chewing on unauthorized items (such as furniture, people and parts
of your home).

TRUTH: If you think that's what *really* happens in actual life, then
there's a very strong possibility that you *may* in fact be from another planet. Puppies *actually* chew on whatever you can't *stop* them from chewing
on.

Almost every chew toy available has some kind of drawback.
Traditional favorites like rawhide can cause digestive blockages if large
chunks are swallowed. Plus, rawhide imported from many third-world
countries is reputedly treated with toxic chemicals before reaching your
dog's mouth. (I can't confirm this. But why take chances?)

Rubber, plastic and soft vinyl toys can also be ingested in dangerously
large chunks. Same for fleecey soft toys. And rope toys.

Toys with bells and squeakers inside also pose a risk: many puppies try
to perform "squeak-ectomies" on such toys the second they get their teeth
on them. And squeakers and bells can cause problems if swallowed.

Some vets warn that real bones may possibly break teeth. And the wrong kind of bones can splinter. What are the wrong kinds? *All* chicken, turkey and pork bones, and *all* beef bones *other* than leg-bones, which are the only ones too tough for dogs to destroy. Sharp shards can do major damage if ingested.

So what's a safe toy policy? Avoid cheap flimsy toys, and then provide your puppy a wide variety of acceptable toys, so she doesn't concentrate on playing with only one kind. This spreads the risk somewhat.

Also, supervise your puppy's play time whenever possible. And monitor the conditions of his toys so you can get rid of damaged and mangled toys before they cause trouble.

That's what we tried to do with Annie and Hawkeye.

But they *still* chewed holes in our kitchen walls.

Yep. *Holes. In walls.*

This happened during the first year we had them, when (as you already know) they were confined to the kitchen when we weren't home or couldn't keep an eye on them.

We don't know who started this culinary custom. We suspected Hawkeye as the initiator because of the altitude of the first toothmarks. Annie was simply too short to reach that high without a great deal of trouble. But she did contribute, and later started her own holes at a comfortable height.

At first, we saw the damage after the fact. So we grumbled about not being able to scold them because we hadn't caught them doing it. We tried using Bitter Apple liquid again. The effects weren't long-lasting enough to dissuade the doggies from resuming their new hobby: wall-chewing.

Although *chewing* isn't really the right word. It was more like *gnawing*. They used their tiny-but-sharp front teeth to nibble at the surface of the walls. It apparently didn't take them long to break through to the "marrow"—the plaster-like core that gives typical drywall its heft and solidity. For reasons we never figured out, they would cut through the surface and keep going, deep inside.

Then they started doing this in more than one spot. The Bitter Apple didn't help. Finally, we caught them in the act. This was major destruction they were doing, and we met it with roars of disapproval. In addition, this was one of the few times we ever grabbed them by the scruffs of their necks and gave them a good shake as we yelled right into their very startled faces.

We realized if we didn't stop this behavior, we'd have a really big problem—*no kitchen walls!* When we moved out, the apartment management folks would likely have noticed. So we brought out the big gun— Tabasco sauce again. We painted it all around the craters the dogs had already made. Then we put some on a paper towel and held it right in front of each dog's nose. One sniff was enough to convince poor Hawkeye that he wanted no part of the stuff.

Annie the skeptic actually insisted on tasting it before she, too, made a *Yuckkk* face. And that's how we stopped them from remodeling our entire kitchen. To be on the safe side, we left the Tabasco sauce on the walls for months, as a reminder intended to discourage new excavations.

Tabasco sauce can be quite decorative, actually, especially if you paint little designs with it. You don't believe that, do you? Nevertheless, we didn't clean and repair the walls until we were quite certain the pups wouldn't take up wall-carving again.

Rules

* It's ultra-important to establish *firm rules* for puppies the day they come to live with us. Puppies are incredibly determined little critters, and they will *try* to get away with what whatever we *allow* them to get away with.

* What's more, they'll try and try and try and try...

* To keep your puppy from chewing on you or your furniture, you must be vigilant—and prepared to correct your puppy's behavior *every single time*.

* Immediately give him a toy he can chew on—and praise him for proper behavior. Every time you let your pup win one of these battles, it makes him even bolder the next time.

* Every time you correct—not *punish*—your pup, you're teaching him by positive action how you want him to behave.

Annie taught me...

It doesn't hurt to be consistent, reliable and fair in all facets of life—not just dog training!

Doors & Gates II:
Annie Houdini

So, we've established that, as a playmate, the kitchen gate wasn't so bad. But as a *gate*, Annie still hated it for depriving her of the freedom to come and go as she chose. And she eventually overcame it through cunning, determination, and a prodigious display of strength.

Here's how.

For almost three years, Cindi and I would go to work in the morning, leaving Hawkeye and Annie in the kitchen—behind that loathsome construction of wood and hardware.

Whoever got home first would let the dogs out and then they'd be free to roam the apartment, as long as someone was there to keep an eye on them.

One evening, I got home—and found Annie waiting for me just inside the front door. I figured Cindi must've come home before me. As I came through our little foyer, I called out a hello to her...and got no reply. She wasn't home.

Not only that, but Hawkeye was still in the kitchen. Behind the closed gate. Yet, somehow, little Annie had escaped. A mystery worthy of Sherlock Holmes.

Next day. Same scenario. True, Annie had done no damage to the apartment during the time she'd been loose. But there was that nagging question of just *how* she was getting out. And the annoying reality that Annie was outsmarting us.

That second night, Annie tipped her hand... er, paw... no, hand.

After we put the dogs in the kitchen at bedtime, we heard a noise. We got up to find Annie prying at the bottom of the gate with her nose. Remember, we had the single latch near the *top* of the gate—which left some "give" at the *bottom*. Annie had figured this out. With a little experimentation, she found she could move the bottom corner enough to squeeze through and escape.

Ah-ha! Now that we knew her secret, how hard could it be to foil her strategy? The obvious solution was to cut off her

Annie and the hated gate: talk about sticking your neck out!

angle of approach. So we took a two-foot-tall decorative barrel we'd been

31

using as an umbrella stand, put it in the kitchen and loaded twenty pounds of dumbbell weights into it. We placed the barrel directly and firmly against that vulnerable gate corner. If she couldn't get to it, she wouldn't be able to open it.

The next evening, I came home—and found Annie happily running around the apartment, and poor frustrated Hawkeye still in the kitchen behind the locked gate. Annie had simply shoved the weighted barrel out of the way. I wondered how early in the day she'd made her break. So I put both dogs in the kitchen, put the barrel back and shut the gate. Then I went outside.

I returned two minutes later—and found that Annie was already out. Apparently, she'd been making her great escapes as soon as the familiar sound of my footsteps faded into the distance outdoors. It was going to take more than twenty pounds to stop this determined Corgi.

So I went out to the local home-improvement store. And came home with a twenty-pound patio paving-brick. We added the brick to the dumbbells. Okay, let's see her move *forty pounds*.

Next evening, there was Annie, running around the apartment.

So it was back to the store for yet *another* patio brick. We added that one to the barrel, which *we* could barely move by now. *Sixty pounds!*

The next evening, I came home. And there was Annie, grinning as she met me at the door. That twenty-two pound, one-foot-tall dog had moved a *sixty pound barrel with her nose*. At that point, all we could do was laugh—and surrender. Annie had won the blessings of liberty for herself and her pal Hawkeye.

From that day on, they had the run of the apartment even when we were gone all day. They never did even the tiniest bit of damage. So maybe the barrel affair was Annie's way of telling us it was time for us to trust them.

Annie taught me...

Obstacles may not be as insurmountable as they appear.

More Games

The smarter the dogs, the more creative they are in the ways they play. Smart dogs will initiate play with you, by bringing over a ball or chew toy and inviting you to join in.

Smart dogs will also figure out amazing ways to entertain themselves, as Annie did with Corgi Punchball. But that wasn't the only game she invented. Among her usual toys were these balls, each made of a long ribbon of rawhide, interwoven to create a roughly round shape, about the size of a tennis ball. Annie loved rawhide and she'd immediately start gnawing, trying to free up an "end." Normally, dogs dismantle and eventually swallow chunks of rawhide. But Annie had another idea.

As soon as she managed to work loose a length of the rawhide strip, instead of chewing it off, she'd use it as a handle. She'd grip it in her mouth and hurl the ball across the room or high up in the air. And then she'd run after it, pounce on it, and throw it again. Pure joy.

One time, as Annie raced around the apartment, tossing and chasing, I heard an alarmingly loud noise from the kitchen. When I went in, I found Annie standing there, looking frustrated. The ball had landed with a *crash!* on top of the stove.

Good thing there wasn't a pot of pasta cooking up there. That rawhide would have been one tough meatball.

Food I: Love at First Bite... and Second and Third

To say that Annie loved food (other than Tabasco sauce) is a little like saying Juliet loved Romeo. Fortunately, Annie's passion for almost anything remotely edible never ended badly. But it did lead to a dizzying variety of adventures and misadventures, all with the same goal: to fill her tummy.

Annie gobbled. Hawkeye picked. Annie swallowed seemingly without chewing. Hawkeye pondered every morsel before munching further. These opposite eating styles caused an obvious conflict.

When *her* bowl was empty, Annie felt compelled to assist Hawkeye in disposing of *his* food.

To avoid fights, we almost immediately started feeding Annie in the large metal-cage crate that served as her bedroom until she was housebroken. Using the crate as her dining room not only solved our problem about Annie raiding Hawkeye's bowl. It also reinforced that the crate was a nice place to be, not a prison.

Of course, Hawkeye's food dish sat only inches away from the crate. And of course Annie tried to extrude herself between the bars to get at all that extra food *almost* within reach of her tongue. But once the crate's door was latched, there was no way out. Hawkeye's food was safe for him to eat, at his own leisurely pace.

After a few weeks of being fed in there, Annie accepted the enforced separation. Not gracefully, mind you. She'd lie flat on her belly, her nose pressed up against the crate bars, pointed at Hawkeye's dish like a compass needle pegged to true north.

One day, many hours before dinnertime, we looked around the apartment for Annie and couldn't find her. Then we looked in the kitchen. She'd stuck her talented little nose in the crate's door handle, unlatched it, and strolled on into her "dining room." There she sat, with an expectant look on her face. Obviously, she was hoping we were sufficiently well-trained by that time to grasp the concept that if she was inside the crate, it *had* to be time to feed her. Just a

Nothing sadder than an empty supper dish. It took sturdy steel bars to keep Annie from inhaling Hawkeye's food as well as hers

few months old, and she was not only smart, but so observant about her environment and the way things worked that we began to suspect she was actually a little person in a doggie suit.

Home Sweet Home

If you start from day-one, it's not hard to get puppies to like (or at least tolerate) their crates. And it's worth the effort to get your puppy to willingly enter her crate on command.

❧ The trick is to help your pup make positive associations with the crate (food, treats, special toys, praise) and not negative ones (loneliness, punishment, separation)

❧ There are lots of ways to accomplish this. For more about getting your pup to think of her crate as a favorite place to hang out (second only to being by your side), read **Crates Are Great!** on page 160.

Annie taught me...

Little creatures—puppies and humans—
need supervision. Judicious limitations on
liberty are part of growing up. If you're
in charge, apply them carefully and fairly—
and everybody wins.

Food II:
Corgi-cules

What's a Corgi-cule?

It's the smallest particle of food still discernible to the nose and/or eyes of a Welsh Corgi—and often *too small* to be detected by humans (or, possibly, even by electron microscopes). Annie spent much of her life searching for them.

Whenever we visited my parents' home, Annie would charge in the front door and rush right to the kitchen. Now, I've gotta tell you, my mother's always been a pretty ship-shape housekeeper. Crumbs, spills and other assorted domestic messes were not permitted to linger in Mom's kitchen.

Yet, skeptic that she was, Annie never took that fact at face value. Instead, she would inspect every corner of the kitchen, looking for... Corgi-cules! At first, I think my mother was a tad offended that anyone— even a dog—might think for the slightest instant that her kitchen was less than spotless.

Inevitably, Anne would find *something* in some crevice inaccessible even to modern vacuum cleaners. And she'd clean it up. So my mother soon came to regard Annie the Inspector not as a critic, but more as an ally against evil crumbs lurking about. Mom recognized that her kitchen was cleaner thanks to Annie's unceasing labors.

Food III:
Explosive Food

The funniest thing I ever saw Annie eat was a cherry tomato. One day, there I was, making a nice summer salad. As usual, Annie hovered just behind me, keeping a sharp eye on the proceedings. She regarded it as her sacred duty to keep any and all food from escaping the premises. If anything leapt to the floor, she'd eat it first and ask questions later.

This particular evening, a plump cherry tomato got loose. Before I could grab it, it rolled off the counter and fell to the floor. Annie pounced!

She got that little tomato completely into her mouth, bit down hard— and was rewarded with a juicy explosion of pulp and seeds filling her mouth. The surprised look on her face was priceless.

To her credit, she didn't lose so much as a single dribble, swallowed the thing, and ate future errant cherry tomatoes with absolute aplomb.

Training I:
My Mistakes, Not Annie's

Cindi and I wanted well-trained dogs. They didn't have to be obedience champions (although Hawkeye later achieved high obedience honors on the dog-show circuit).

We did want them to learn what was okay to do, and what wasn't. No biting, not even playfully. No jumping on people, even in a friendly way. No destruction of anything other than approved chew toys. They had to come when called, and obey basic commands like sit, stay and down.

All these fell under the overall category of what I call "manners." We wanted our pups to be reliable and well-behaved enough so they'd be good, trouble-free company for us and our friends and relatives. We also wanted them to be welcome in other people's homes and in public places.

To accomplish this, we enrolled both puppies in obedience classes not long after we got them. Cindi had had dogs while she was growing up, so she already had a working knowledge of basic training. I, on the other hand, knew nothing but the theories absorbed from reading a few training books and pamphlets. I had no practical experience. And I soon learned the real value of formal obedience classes is to train the *owner*, not the *dog*.

There are several training alternatives. Many professional trainers offer one-on-one lessons. This may be expensive, ($40 to $100 an hour) but it's probably the most effective choice. The same trainers often conduct more affordable group classes, too. Many local school districts and recreation departments also offer group classes, as do some pet-supply stores. Obviously, stores hope you'll buy something before you leave. But that doesn't have to detract from the potential value of the training.

Compare classes before you sign up. Ask for a brochure or class curriculum. Try to talk to the trainer and get a feel for style and personality. Some are drill-sergeants, while others try to make puppy school fun.

Look for classes limited to a dozen pups or less. More than that, and you may get lost in the crowd. Even in a group class, trainers should try to give *some* individual attention to everyone. However, even the best trainer can't be everywhere at once. So don't expect undivided attention. And any time a bunch of untrained puppies and novice owners get together, a certain level of chaos is to be expected.

But these classes can still be worthwhile. For one thing, your pup gets a chance to socialize with other dogs on neutral turf. You'll get to see how your pet reacts in an environment full of distractions. And even if your puppy-student doesn't learn much, *you* should be able to learn the techniques *you'll* need to train your own dog on your own time.

These techniques aren't hard, although you'll certainly have doubts when your puppy seems to be doing everything but learning how to behave.

The key is kindly repetition. Don't try to train your dog when either of you is tired and snappish. *Do* train your dog when you're both happy and fresh. And do it in short stints. Even the biggest of puppies have miniature attention spans. If they get bored or cranky, they're not going to obey or listen, and you'll end up very frustrated.

I know this because I committed every mistake possible. At the time I got Annie, I worked in New York City. By the time I commuted home to the suburbs on the Long Island Railroad, scarfed down a quick dinner and got ready to take her to puppy class, I was tired. When Annie inevitably didn't follow instructions, I got cranky.

And we both ended up unhappy.

After a few weeks, I decided to make a concerted effort at "home-schooling." I set aside a

---

A Teacher's Touch

- ❧ Yes, it helps to know certain basic techniques in order to train your puppy. But patience and love are just as important.

- ❧ You and your pup will both make mistakes. So don't expect miracles when you start training.

- ❧ Do expect progress.

- ❧ Dogs love to be loved. So be generous with praise. Our pups may not be perfect—but neither are we! Perfect or not, let your dog know you appreciate her efforts.

- ❧ Try to end every training session on a high note. Success really does breed success.

few minutes here and there, trying to do at least some training every day. That worked out pretty well. Annie began to make noticeable progress in developing those all-important manners.

Annie taught me...

To be a good teacher, it helps to be a good student. Pay attention, see your student's point of view, and keep your sense of humor. Life is serious enough: learning should be fun!

Training II:
Honking Her Own Horn

A few months later, Cindi signed both puppies up at more advanced classes offered by a local dog club. I admit she was more motivated and energetic than I was (and she still is).

She signed Hawkeye up for intermediate classes and Annie for beginners. They were held at consecutive hours in the same location. She'd take one dog in at a time and leave the other out in the car.

One night, while Hawkeye was going through his paces inside, the whole class heard a car horn honking out in the parking lot. *Repeatedly.* When Cindi came out, she found Annie in the driver's seat, jumping up and pounding the horn with her little hands. Where other puppies might have been scared by the sudden loud noise, Annie had apparently figured out that *she* was causing the noise. She didn't like being cooped up in the car, away from the action. So she kept honking.

Training III:
Torture By Treats

It quickly became clear to us that Annie was an exceptionally bright student. Once we figured out how to communicate something to her, she'd learn it almost instantly. It also became clear that a time-honored and effective training strategy did *not* work with Annie.

I'm talking about treat-rewards. It's simple conditioning: when your dog does what you want her to do, reward her with a small food morsel. Many trainers use cut-up hot dogs. Others use dry kibble-type food. Food-reward training is widely used by professionals who train everyday dogs to do amazing and funny stunts for television, movies and circus acts.

Why didn't it work with Annie? Because she was so food-oriented that once she knew there were treats in the immediate *hemisphere*, she paid attention only to the food, or to the hand or pocket holding that food. She didn't care what you might be telling her, or asking her to do. All she wanted was that food! Seeing her eyes riveted on your hand or pocket bordered on scary. You could almost see her doggie brain sending out telepathic thought-waves: *Come to me, Food! Come to me!* (Kind of like that intensely-determined "*Yo quiero Taco Bell*" chihuahua in the TV commercials.)

So we quickly abandoned treat-rewards and resorted to another powerful training tool: praise. Annie ate that up with only a smidgen less enthusiasm than she devoted to actual edibles. So it worked for us. The sheer joy she got out of learning something new and knowing we were pleased with her seemed motivation enough.

Training IV:
How's Tricks?

The smarter your dog, the more he needs to be kept busy. If you don't keep him busy, he'll find his own activities to occupy himself. And those may include unraveling your rugs, whittling your woodwork or unstuffing your sofa.

The more positive alternative is for us to pay attention to our pups and engage them in constructive activities, like the aforementioned obedience training. I can't tell you how much better it is to have a dog who knows such basics as *Sit, Down, Stay* and *Come*.

Actually, yes, I can tell you, and I will. It's much better. And there's really no excuse for not training our dogs. It's not that hard. All it takes is patience and a positive attitude.

As nice as it may be to have a pet who minds his basic manners, it's even nicer to have one who learns how to do special things. Yes—*tricks*.

It's not a dirty word. It's not undignified for your dog. In fact, it's great fun for both you and your pet, and gives you something else to do together. And you teach tricks with pretty much the same techniques as obedience training.

In Annie's case, it didn't take her long to learn to hold hands, wave, give kisses, jump obstacles and roll over. It was even more amazing when she learned nuances to some of those tricks.

One day, Cindi and I were watching TV in our living room. Annie was being particularly obnoxious. She taunted Hawkeye. She bugged us. She wanted attention and she wanted it *now!* So, without thinking, Cindi pointed her finger at Annie, pulled the "trigger," and said: "*Bang.*"

At that instant, we looked at each other, laughed, and decided we'd try to teach Annie to lie down, roll belly-up and "play dead" in sequence on the command "Bang." Without really knowing how to do this, we worked on getting Annie to combine those three distinct actions upon hearing the single command. And we were amazed when she learned the new and complex trick within three or four brief training sessions.

Annie remembered how to do "*Bang*" for the rest of her life, no matter how long the interval since her last performance. There were times when she did it grudgingly. But she'd always do it for us, if we asked. And it always got a laugh.

You don't have to teach your dog the tricks Annie learned. But some kind of basic training is imperative. If only there was a way to make sure all prospective dog-owners understood this before they added a dog to their families. Dogs are ideally suited to sharing a home with humans— but only if we help them understand how we want them to behave.

It's appalling to find out the "reasons" some people give for abandoning their pets or dumping them at already overcrowded animal shelters. Sometimes—rarely, I think—there's no other choice. But a huge percentage of the dogs that end up in shelters are there because their owners were too busy, too lazy, or too ignorant to spend even a minimal amount of time and effort training their pets. The more time you put into training when your puppy is young, the more likely you are to have a dog that's a pleasure to have around.

(Of course, some parents appear to be guilty of the same disregard for their children. But that's a topic for another book.)

Sure, there *are* some problem dogs, just as there are problem people. But the average puppy is trainable. If we don't *bother* with training, and the puppy shreds the Persian rug, don't blame the puppy!

Training V:
Learning All Day, Every Day

One of the most important things Annie taught me is that puppies are learning constantly—whether *we're* teaching them or not. Nature has equipped them to observe and remember anything and everything about their immediate environment—*if* it's important to them.

So they quickly learn what times of day they're fed. And they also learn where their food is kept. In our house, we always joke about our dogs worshipping the Holy Pantry from which so much bounty comes. They also learn all the sounds that are important, and what they mean. They learn which sounds mean food is about to be prepared, and which sounds mean the UPS delivery guy is about to come to the door. They learn what your car's engine and door-slam sound like, as opposed to those similar noises coming from your neighbor's car—because *those* sounds mean you're about to arrive at home.

Most trainers and training books strongly recommend that people spend 15 to 30 minutes every day training their young puppies. And I agree.

Unfortunately, reality has a way of disrupting those plans. There will be many days when even the most dedicated dog-owner fails to spend that all-important time on training. If that happens to you on a regular basis, should you feel bad about it?

Well, yes, you *should*. But just because you didn't find 15 minutes to spend exclusively on a formal puppy-training session doesn't mean you don't have time to train your puppy. The fact is, you spend considerably *more* than 15 minutes every day interacting with your pup. Walking, feeding, playing, petting, scolding.

Annie taught me...

Any and all encounters with
your puppy throughout the day
are perfect training opportunities.

This sort of "training" could be something as simple asking your dog to sit before he gets a treat or a toy. Asking him to stay before you'll serve his dinner. Asking him to bring back the toy you've just thrown, and making him drop it before you'll continue playing.

Believe it or not, all those little moments of reinforcement add up over the course of days, weeks and months. Before you know it, your puppy has learned all sorts of things that make him a more pleasant companion.

So, yes, you should try to set aside time every day to teach your puppy the basics of good-doggie manners. But you should also teach yourself to take advantage of all those informal but critical training opportunities that happen every day.

Talking to Your Dog

People don't talk to their dogs enough. And, no, I'm not crazy.

Lots of perfectly reasonable people think that only eccentric old biddies and outright loons talk to dogs. We who know better should be generous, and forgive their ignorance. First off, dogs have very human eyes. Those expressive eyes beg for communication.

Which raises a perfectly reasonable question: do dogs really *understand* a word we say? Or is it more like the classic *"Far Side"* cartoon depicting an owner talking to a dog in complete sentences, captioned *What we say to dogs*. The identical picture is repeated, only this time from the dog's point of view, with the caption *What dogs hear: "Blaah blaah blaah Ginger blaah blaah."* It's a funny comic strip. It's also not true.

One of the books I read when I first got Annie asserted that mature dogs have roughly the comprehension capacity of an average five-year-old child. Before knowing Annie, I would not have believed that. Now I do.

Books on dog training and intelligence give varying estimates on the vocabulary of spoken words and phrases dogs can learn and reliably remember—anywhere from a hundred to several hundred. We never stopped to count Annie's vocabulary. There wasn't much point, since she seemed to understand almost everything we said to her.

Obviously, she didn't get every word. But just as obviously, she learned all the words and phrases that were important to her and helped her navigate her way through life. She not only knew isolated words, like *eat*; she also knew the phrases that commonly contained those words. If you say *"eat"* in association with feeding, your dog will learn the word. With Annie, I would usually say, "Annie, do you want to eat?" By now, you know Annie's answer was always affirmative.

By using *"Do you want…"* as the prelude, we also got her to react positively to that phrase alone, even if the last word wasn't *"eat."* Now, I'm not claiming any great discovery here. Since she first associated the introductory phrase with "...eat," it was only natural she'd express interest at hearing "*do you want...*" Would she react the same way to "*Do you want...to discuss the philosophical impact of existentialism on contemporary literature?*" as she would to "*Do you want... to play in the mud?*" Probably.

But the point is, by regularly using actual English phrases when you talk to your dog, she'll develop the ability to comprehend conversational language as opposed to the baby-talk reverted to by many pet owners. Maybe it's just me, but I'd find it a whole lot less embarrassing to be overheard saying to my dog, "Annie, do you want to go for a walk?" than "Ooooh! Widdle puppy go for walkums?"

When Dogs Talk Back

If you spend enough time with dogs, you'll find out many of them talk. I don't mean simple barking. They vocalize in ways that are both very funny and very communicative.

One of our current Corgis, Mickey, does what we call "singin' the blues." It often happens when my wife Susan comes home from work. Mickey is a fluffy dog with a sweet innocence about her. If she had a motto, it would be "Meandering to a Different Drummer." Mickey does not guard her emotions closely. Whether it's joy or desolation, Mickey puts everything on display. If anyone still thinks dogs don't have emotions, spend a little time with our Mickey.

For most of our day, Mickey is pretty quiet. But when my wife Susan drives up, Mickey revs up. When Susan comes upstairs from the garage, Mickey is right there to greet her. Mick throws her head back, and howls out her troubles: "Oh mommy I had such a hard day Daddy didn't pet me enough and sister Callie was a brat and I missed you so much..."

And all we can do is laugh.

Annie wasn't as sensitive or demonstrative as little Mick. And by now, you know that Annie had this definite dominant streak. She wanted what she wanted, and she wanted it *now*! If you were too slow, or had somehow displeased her, she would assume this impatient posture that had to be the canine equivalent of putting hands on hips. Then you would get what was very clearly a scolding. Her mouth would move as if she was about to talk—in real English. What would come out was, "*Rrowwrrowwrrooowwrrr.*"

In any language, it was disgruntled grumbling. Susan eventually coined a perfectly descriptive verb for what Annie did: *grunteling*.

Dance of the Doggie Hormones

I never intended to breed Annie. And I knew it was the responsible thing to have her spayed. Years later, I also learned that neutering both male and female dogs can help them avoid a whole assortment of potentially serious medical conditions as they grow older. I just wasn't sure when would be the right time to take care of this.

Annie and Hawkeye told us when.

It happened right around the time Annie was five months old. Hawk was a month older. Cindi and I were minding our own business in our living room while the puppies played with their chew toys and bones. Suddenly, Annie let out a shriek of alarm that made us rush over. Had Hawkeye accidentally bitten her?

Annie cowered in angry terror. Poor Hawkeye looked totally befuddled. There wasn't a mark on Annie. Not even a drop of Hawk-spit. Nothing at all to indicate he'd so much as touched her. So we shrugged and went back to our respective activities.

Same thing happened later on. This time, we reacted quickly enough to notice that Hawkeye was sniffing Annie's little bunny-butt rear end in a new way—to which she objected very strenuously. He was just doing what came naturally, apparently sensing a difference about her that only a dog would notice. We deduced that Annie was starting to go through the hormonal changes that sent unmistakable signals to her male playmate.

We wondered for a moment about the odd combinations we might get if a Corgi and Collie had kids. Little noses, short legs, long tails. Big noses, little legs. Little noses, long legs...etc.

. But before any unplanned puppies came our way, we had Annie spayed. And she and Hawkeye went back to being buddies.

Mail Order Annie, Attorney-at-Law

None of the training books I read prepared me for having a dog that would distinguish between the *letter* of the law and the *spirit*.

For most of the three years that Cindi, Hawkeye, Annie and I shared our little apartment, the dogs slept in the kitchen. With the gate closed. It was just a continuation of the habit we'd established back during their puppyhood. They were content to sleep in the same room, sometimes together, sometimes apart. And confinement meant they couldn't get into any overnight trouble beyond that one room.

The bedtime ritual included potty walks, some petting, and then the word "*bedtime*." As the dogs quickly learned, that meant it was time to go into the kitchen and go to sleep. As they got a little older, they also learned what "*Everybody into the kitchen*" meant, and they'd do as they were told.

Normally, when Cindi or I said that sentence, Hawkeye obediently went in and found a corner in which to bed down. Annie followed, waited until he was comfy, and then snuggled in his tail.

In many ways, adult dogs are like little kids. They know what they're supposed to do, but every now and then they'll test the limits, just to make sure they still have to do it.

So, one night, Annie decided—kid-style—that she didn't want to go to bed when told to do so. In her mind, it was time to take a stand, to split hairs over the phrase "*Everybody into the kitchen*." Instead of simply following Hawkeye in, Annie set one front paw over the threshold, as if to say, "*There, I'm in*." Then she turned and scampered back into the living room.

Plainly, she was counting on one of two miracles to happen: either we wouldn't notice, or we'd concur with her interpretation of the law. We did not concur. I responded to her non-verbal argument with a stern look, and the phrase "*All the way in*." Annie reacted with a moment of defiance. Then she hung her head, lowered her expressive ears and shambled into the kitchen. *All the way in.*

Had she been able to write, I'm sure Annie would have filed cogent briefs with the proper legal authorities. If need be, she would have pursued her case all the way to the Supreme Court, proud to be the first Welsh Corgi to argue before that august body. As it was, as long as she was required to sleep in the kitchen, she made repeated appeals in the only way she could—by forcing me to say "*All the way in*" virtually every night.

I don't know if all dogs grasp such nuances of language, but Annie sure did.

Poop Patrol

Okay. Here's an embarrassing question: Do you pick up after your dog?

The smelly truth is, too many of us don't. You only have to look around in areas where dogs take their walks to see the proof. Too many dog owners don't realize that nothing gives us the right to "foul the footpaths" (as the British say).

And this happens despite the fact that, in many urban and suburban municipalities, failure to pick up after your pet happens to be a punishable offense. Never mind the additional and indisputable fact that it also happens to be gross, disgusting and a health hazard to litter the landscape with poop piles.

Raise your-hand if you've never in your life stepped in dog poop. Or never had your child step in it. Hmm, I see a few lucky souls out there. But the vast majority of us *have* had the pleasure of trying to clean off our shoe bottoms (really fun with modern athletic shoes, with all the nooks and crannies in their convoluted sculpted soles).

I freely confess that I am a reformed sinner. For the first few years I had Annie, I would guiltily leave behind whatever she left behind. I was fully aware that I was doing something wrong. But I did it anyway. I would justify it by thinking, *Well, it's only along the fence of the apartment property. Nobody actually walks there.*

We also had a fenced-in former playground on the apartment's property, its concrete surface broken, overgrown with weeds, swing-sets and see-saws long since removed. This had become a de facto dog run for our entire apartment complex. Tenants took their dogs there, letting them off-leash to play and poop as they pleased.

Well, eventually, the private homeowners living on either side complained about the stink rising from this old playground in hot weather. And the apartment maintenance men had long complained of having to mow lawns that had become poop-laden minefields. So the management finally got tough and informed dog-owning tenants in no uncertain terms that we had to pick up after our pets, or face consequences.

So, I was shamed into compliance. And I discovered it was neither awful nor difficult to be a good citizen. You don't need fancy or cumbersome scoopers. All you need is plastic bags. Some people use grocery bags, or the plastic sleeves in which our newspapers are home-delivered.

However, sometimes these used bags have small holes in them, which may not be discovered until it's too late. So I prefer to buy bulk quantities of simple 1-gallon freezer-type bags. They're sold at any grocery store, in boxes of 75 or 150, so they cost a penny or two per bag. And I never leave the house without several stuffed into my pocket.

Here's the simplest clean-up technique: Place the bag over your hand like a glove. Pick up the poop (carefully). Invert the bag. Tie off the top of the bag. *Voila!* Done. Then toss the thing in a separate outdoor trash bag, and get rid of a week's worth with the regular trash pick-up.

I haven't come across many (any?) trainers who actively campaign to get dog-owners to observe this matter of common sense and common courtesy. It really is important. In my group puppy-obedience classes, I try to mention this issue in our first meeting, when I do a people-only briefing, without puppies present. Once, I forgot to give them the speech during the first session.

During the second class, one of the puppies pooped. The owner hadn't brought any bags, so I gave him one. And then I reminded the class to always pick up after their dogs, and to bring bags to class. Well, the following week, when the first puppy of the day pooped, that owner found herself being offered spare bags by *everyone* in the class. I had a proud moment.

So, please do the right thing with *your* dog.

Annie taught me...

If we don't clean up our messes (literal and figurative), we eventually step in them.

Dogs Never Forget

When Annie and Hawkeye were three, Cindi and her trusty Collie moved to California. People and canines alike missed each other. But at least people can understand *why* their pals have gone away.

Annie only understood that her adopted brother and her "mommy" Cindi went out and didn't came back. And Annie's loneliness broke my heart. She moped for months. The only thing I could do was spend more time

Kim hugs Hawkeye goodbye shortly before he moved to California

47

with her. And a new roommate moved in—another set of hands to pet her.

But I don't think she ever got over losing Hawkeye. She never befriended another dog. And for the rest of her life, she approached Collies differently than other dogs. Whenever she saw a Collie, she'd pull me toward it, as if wondering: "It looks like Hawkeye. Maybe it is." When she'd get close enough for a proper sniff, she'd know it wasn't.

When Hawkeye got to California after driving cross-country in Cindi's brand-new Chevy Blazer, he acquired a "pet" of his own—a kitten named Buddy. And all of Hawkeye's sweet, gentle nature came out. Hawk regarded Buddy as his baby, letting the kitten snuggle up to him.

And he'd also lick Buddy the way he used to lick Annie's ears. Except Buddy was pretty tiny, and his ears were even more tiny. So Hawk would lick the entire cat. And when Cindi went to pet or pick up her kitten, she'd find him sopping wet.

Annie and Hawkeye saw each other once after Cindi and her dog moved to California. About six months later, they came back to visit friends and family. It was Christmastime, and all the boarding kennels in the Los Angeles area were booked solid. So Cindi had no choice but to take Hawkeye and Buddy back east with her on the overnight flight.

They arrived without mishap. Cindi packed the dog and cat crates into a rental car and drove up to our old Westbury apartment just as I was taking Annie out for her morning walk. When Annie saw them, she exploded with joy and rushed up to greet her long-lost friends. Poor Hawkeye had been sedated for the flight, and he was still pretty wobbly. Annie nearly knocked him over.

Once we brought them inside, Hawkeye found his old-favorite corner in the kitchen and promptly fell asleep. And it didn't take long for Annie to find *her* favorite sleeping place: resting with her face buried in Hawkeye's bushy tail

Just like old times.

Annie welcomes Hawkeye home, if only for a visit

Cats

As I mentioned, Buddy the cat made the cross-country trip, too. I was a little leery of having a cat in the apartment. For a couple of reasons.

First, I'm just not a cat-person. I don't mean to offend anyone who is. I can appreciate cats as natural marvels, both as beautiful objects and functional creatures. I can even understand why lots of people love cats. I'm just not one of those people.

I have no doubts that cats are intelligent. I have no idea if dogs are smarter than cats, or vice versa. I have no idea how you'd even measure such a contest. Even though I love dogs and can live without cats, I don't feel a need to prove that dogs are smarter. It really doesn't matter.

I will merely say this to both cat and dog people who are compelled to assert the intellectual superiority of one species over the other: *Get a life!*

Dogs and cats *are* what they *are*. And I'm about to generalize here, so don't shoot me, or sue me.

By nature, cats seem to be solitary creatures. They don't generally hang out in cooperative packs as dogs and their wild cousins do, and as canine ancestors did.

I've been around enough cats to have observed that they tend to be unpredictable. Maybe it's because I don't know them well, but I can't tell whether any given cat is going to be friendly—or claw me. In general, cats seem to play their emotional cards close to the vest, as if Nature has taught them the advantages of surprise. Neither cats' faces nor their body language seem to be as outwardly expressive as those of dogs.

Dogs, by contrast, are hopeless *blabbermouths* when it comes to body language and facial expressions. It's a rare dog that doesn't instantly react and reveal. You don't have to possess a doctorate in animal behavior to look at almost any dog and make a reasonable guess as to whether the animal is fearful or joyful, vicious or friendly.

I've known lots of people with cats. And more often than not, when I visit their homes, the cats are nowhere to be seen. Cats seem to seek solitude.

Dogs, on the other hand, rush to the door to announce and greet.

Plus, cats are tough to train. Not impossible, mind you, but tough. As a result, most cat owners don't even bother trying to train their pets. As a further result, cats do what they want and go where they please.

Cats are notorious for climbing drapes and levitating onto kitchen counters and tables. The idea of pets walking on food-preparation surfaces doesn't thrill me. (I'd be equally unthrilled by dogs doing the same thing.) There's not a whole lot you can do to stop cats from being cats—especially when you're not home to witness these acts of cat-ness.

But the main reason cats and I just don't click is emotional. Even (some) cat lovers will admit that their pets frequently behave like they can take or leave human company. The typical dog wants nothing more than to be with the people who make up its surrogate pack. I already endure enough feline-like indifference from *actual people*. I don't need more of it from *animal* companions. So that's why I prefer the company of dogs.

End of generalizations. I *know* there are dogs who act more like cats, and cats who seem to think they're dogs. But those are the exceptions.

Okay. So that's why I was leery of having Buddy-cat come to visit. Annie had her own reasons.

Remember the day Annie and I chose each other at her breeder's house? Remember her reaction to the resident cat? I don't know what that cat did, but all of Annie's subsequent encounters with cats made it clear she'd never forgotten her early skirmishes with the feline Lord of the Hillendale kitchen. Put a cat in her path and she'd snarl and strain at her leash like she wanted to even some long-simmering score. Her rabid-wolf act usually had the desired effect: the cats made hasty exits.

But I needed to know: was Annie really all bark and no bite as I'd begun to suspect? What would she do if she really got up-close-and-personal with a cat? One tough-looking cat that hung out in and around our apartment building gave me the chance to find out.

On this particular occasion, we ran into this big striped cat parked on the entry stoop. Annie did her usual sound and tooth show. And I

Annie and Buddy give each other the once-over

shocked her by not pulling back on her leash. I didn't let her go, of course, but I did allow some slack. Presented with a new situation, Annie seemed caught off-guard. With rather more caution than I expected, she sniffed toward the cat.

The cat didn't like this at all. His personal space invaded, he slashed out with one front paw. This time, it was Annie's turn to flinch.

Obviously, the cat didn't feel like cooperating and the experiment ended with me shooing the cat away and hustling Annie inside. Only then did I notice a couple of razor slices across her nose. I felt like an idiot for exposing her to greater potential harm—what if the cat had reached her eye? I doctored Annie's nose and promised her we'd steer clear of cats in the future.

Which we did, until Buddy accompanied Hawkeye and Cindi on their Christmas trip back east. While Hawkeye wobbled into the apartment on legs still rubbery from his sedative, Cindi carried Buddy in, still inside his travel crate. She put the crate down, set up his litter box, and opened his little door.

Buddy refused to come out. He'd been crammed into a cramped box for the better part of a day, and he was *cranky*. I can't say I blamed him. His hissing let us know he was also less than ecstatic about this strange dog—Annie—sticking her nose into his carrier.

But there was no overt hostility on the part of either animal. So we decided to let them sort out the situation in their own way.

Eventually, Buddy emerged, on high alert. Since the cat was declawed, there wasn't much chance of Annie getting injured. And Buddy wasn't in great danger either. Even if Annie decided to try taking a chunk out of him, cats can go places dogs can't—such as, straight up. So we reasoned that Buddy would be able to escape if he had to.

As it turned out, *both* animals surprised us. Their reactions to each other were surprisingly mild. Buddy remained defensive. Annie was simply curious. After a while, the cat felt secure enough to let Annie approach and sniff him. And Annie came to the conclusion that Buddy posed no threat.

By the time Hawkeye slept off the last effects of his drugs, Annie and Buddy had become uneasy playmates. Soon after, as the three of them romped together, Annie realized this cat had some advantages over the bigger dog: Buddy could fit under the same furniture as Annie.

The games began with the dogs chasing the cat. Buddy had quickly sized up the apartment. He knew which chairs, couches, tables and counters were available for evasive maneuvers. So he allowed himself to thoroughly enjoy playtime.

At a certain point in the chase, Buddy raced under the living room loveseat. Annie charged in after him. For a cartoonish moment, neither animal came out. There was just the sound of momentary scuffling—for position only, since there were no screeches, growls or howls of distress. Then the animals flew back out—but with Annie as *pursued* and Buddy as *pursuer*! They raced around some more,

Buddy-cat looks like he's making an editorial comment about having to spend a week away from home, with not one but TWO dogs

under and over all manner of obstacles. Poor Hawkeye whimpered in frustration because he couldn't follow Buddy and Annie through all the small spaces included in the game. The chase route took them back under the loveseat, with Annie diving in first and Buddy right behind. As before, when they came out, they'd reversed positions. They'd invented a game they played joyfully throughout Buddy's week-long stay.

Over the next few days, Buddy impressed me with his adaptability. Among his useful discoveries, he found he could fit on the kitchen windowsill, and he took advantage of southern exposure to the December sun. He also discovered he could fit through the gaps in the kitchen gate when it was closed. So, while the dogs could be confined, Buddy was free to roam.

By using his new knowledge of his temporary surroundings, Buddy invented his own game. One day, all three animals were in the kitchen, with the gate closed. Buddy sunned himself on the window sill, and Hawkeye rested. Annie lay on her belly, her nose stuck through the gate and her chin resting on the bottom rail.

Suddenly, Buddy leaped from his perch, skipped across the kitchen floor, bounced onto Annie's back and slipped through the gate before startled Annie could even react.

Buddy apparently found this highly entertaining, because he repeated his prank several times before he left. Poor Annie never did figure out effective countermeasures. Our reunion week passed quickly. It had been fun, for both people and animals. When Cindi and her pets left us, I think Annie actually missed that little cat.

Annie the TV Analyst

Dogs perceive the world differently than we do. In general, their senses and powers of observation are much sharper than those of humans. Such are the natural gifts bequeathed by their wild wolf ancestors. Experts think canine noses are hundreds of times more sensitive than ours. (Humorist Dave Barry refers to the Beagle, noted in particular for its olfactory prowess, as "biologically, a nose with feet.")

Their hearing is better, too. Which is why we don't need to yell at our dogs when we're mad at them. A conversational growl does quite nicely, thank you.

And though they don't process vivid colors as we do, their eyes are uniquely designed to see well in low light and to detect motion—advantageous qualities when ancient canines had to hunt for food. Even though modern pet dogs don't have much opportunity or need to catch prey, those ancestral reflexes are hard-wired into their brains. That's why our dogs love to pounce upon every skittering leaf on blustery autumn days, why a plastic bag blown by a summer breeze triggers a barking frenzy, and why a scurrying squirrel simply *must* be chased.

Which leads us to a significant question eventually pondered by almost everyone who owns a dog: do dogs watch television? And if they do, what do they see?

I remember the first time Annie showed substantial interest in a TV show. I was watching a public-television show about cats, both big and wild and small and domestic. During one segment, a tabby cat appeared onscreen and meowed rather loudly. Well, Annie's ears sure did perk up! And as I watched her, I could see her try to figure out an anomaly: the sound and picture didn't quite match.

This was before I had a stereo television, so the set had one small speaker in the lower-right front corner. The cat appeared dead-center on the screen, but the *sound* of the cat clearly originated elsewhere, and Annie's right radar-dish ear swiveled to home in upon what she *knew* to be the source of the meow.

To make the situation even more confusing, this cat didn't smell like a cat. In fact, it didn't smell like anything.

Then Annie did something that truly amazed me. Taking action both analytical yet literal, she stepped to one side of the TV, then the other, peering behind it on both sides. She was obviously trying to find the rest of the two-dimensional cat on the screen, figuring it had to be somewhere behind the "window." When she couldn't find the back of the cat, couldn't smell the cat, and couldn't quite figure out why the cat's voice wasn't coming out of its mouth, I guess she concluded the cat must be inside the "box." This seemed to satisfy her, and she decided there was no need to be concerned about this particular cat.

Another program that regularly attracted Annie's attention—and is also watched closely by Mickey and Callie, Annie's Welsh Corgi successors— is CBS's classy *Sunday Morning*, long hosted by the late, great Charles Kuralt. Each week, *Sunday Morning* always ends with a minute or two of scenic footage from all kinds of wilderness settings. These tranquil interludes are accompanied by neither music nor human voice, only the natural sounds recorded on the spot.

Many of these nature segments include animals going about their lives, and calling out in their many voices. Sometimes, motion alone is enough to get our dogs to watch. But noise really rivets their attention. And the more noise the televised animals make, and the more uncommon their howls, growls, grunts, trumpets and trills may be, the more those amazing Corgi ears twitch and swivel in alert fascination.

Now Playing:
"Attack of the Killer Fleas!"

The summer of '84, the season when Cindi and Hawkeye departed, turned out to be my very own, personal (if somewhat-condensed) version of the biblical Ten Plagues.

There were the fleas, of course.

And the fact that I was under contract to write a novel. Which I kept putting off. Which meant that time slipped away without my having written a word. Which ultimately meant I ended up having a scant six weeks to write the damned thing. Under duress and stress. Which may be pretty much the same thing. But redundancy is quite proper in this instance.

And then there were the fleas.

Since I didn't have a replacement roommate lined up, my cash-flow situation fell to critical condition. I was supposed to be an usher at a best friend's North Carolina wedding, but bowed out at the last minute to save the costs of plane fare, hotel, and tux rental.

Paying for a two-bedroom apartment myself was not going to be feasible in the long term, so I prepared for a possible move to smaller and cheaper quarters. To lighten the load for that eventuality, I started going through my belongings and tossing stuff I hadn't looked at or used in years.

Old books were given away to the library. Old clothing went to the Goodwill drop-box. And then I committed a sin that would later cause wails of grief and gnashing of teeth.

First, a preface to this self-inflicted tragedy. Almost all guys of a certain age share a common horrific experience: the mid-life realization that our mothers *threw out our baseball-card collections* barely seconds after we departed the parental nest and foolishly left childhood treasures behind (usually in a shoebox at the bottom of a closet).

I suppose, if we're in a forgiving mood, we can grudgingly concede that our mothers knew not what they did. I mean, who knew those gum-scented cards, purchased with handfuls of loose change from allowances and paper-routes, would someday be worth real money?

But in the summer of '84, I *myself* committed the crime, which might be called "*Collectible-icide*." I still had a cache of sports memorabilia, rescued from Mom's cleaning clutches—mostly New York Yankees and Mets yearbooks from the early 1960s. Among them were the Mets yearbooks from their epically awful yet historically significant inaugural seasons in '62 and '63. I had also inherited stewardship of a couple of yearbooks originally bought by my older brother, possibly including (I can't be sure;

post-traumatic stress disorder has reduced my memories of this event to a haze of denial) the yearbook from the Dodgers' last season in New York and/or first season in Los Angeles.

And I also had a variety of old Ford automobile literature and brochures that I'd saved since the early '60s.

In a mindless fit of purging, I threw all that stuff out. Compared to the sum total of my belongings, the items I'd judged to be worthless surplus did not even fill a single paper grocery sack. Had I kept it all, it would have taken up, at most, the bottom of one dresser drawer.

But out it went. Can't blame Mom for this one.

Years later, after baby-boomer nostalgia became big business, I discovered at various collectibles shows that those baseball yearbooks had come to be worth as much as fifty bucks each. The Ford brochures and dealer booklets go for similar amounts.

And I learned the hard way that *"Those who do not save the past are doomed to repurchase it."*

And then. Oh yes. There were the fleas.

Let me say right here that most of the anti-flea products on the market at that time were pretty much useless. And the ones that did work tended to be rather toxic.

To say that the flea season began rather abruptly that year would be classic understatement. It literally seemed that one day there were none, and the next day Annie and I found ourselves at the headquarters hotel for the biggest flea convention in history.

Or, to be more accurate, we *were* the headquarters hotel for the biggest flea convention in history. Prior to this, I didn't even know what a flea looked like. I'd just plain never laid eyes on one. Then, just like that, they seemed to be everywhere.

Contrary to what many of us think we learned (probably from cartoons), fleas don't live on animals all the time. They do live just about everywhere else. When a suitable animal host happens by, fleas hop on for a ride and a bite. When they're done, they may stick around, party, have flea-sex (don't ask), lay eggs, develop the next generation, and/or hop off anywhere they please—including inside our homes. Having made it past the front door, they happily set up housekeeping in carpets, sofa cushions, and the nooks and crannies of our floorboards. Once ensconced, they're extremely tough to get rid of.

But they do start outdoors, where ideal flea-spawning conditions include a cool, damp spring followed by a suddenly-hot summer. And that's just what we had that year.

To leave the front door of my apartment building was to run a gantlet manned by countless voracious insects just waiting to pounce. And I learned to my horror that fleas are not picky when it comes to hopping aboard a passing train. Any mammal will do.

I discovered this one evening after rushing Annie back into the apartment, then looking down to see my white pants-legs covered with little black dots. Dots that *moved*. Dots that *jumped off to set up housekeeping*!

At risk of offending folks who believe that all God's creatures were put here for a purpose… *there's no reason for fleas*. They exist solely to plague us and our animals, and to spread infection and disease while they're at it. They bite. They suck blood. They leave tiny, itchy, red welts in their wake. And their saliva can cause maddening allergic reactions.

Now, you may be wondering, "How much flea-spit can there be in something the size of a pin-head?"

Enough. MORE than enough.

By the time I belatedly realized the gravity of our outdoor flea infestation, the little blood-suckers had already established an indoor beachhead. This became more than apparent when I noticed flea-bites on my legs, and then discovered some of the miniscule monsters in my bed.

It wasn't enough that they were terrorizing and torturing Annie, who spent much of her time in a jitterbug-frenzy of biting and scratching. Now the brazen little demons came right after me—*in my BED*!

I had no choice but to declare war.

First line of attack: flea-bombing our apartment. Like the late great Neutron Bomb idea, insecticide bombs kill the offending life forms but leave the building standing.

Theoretically.

Next, I had to come up with a way to avoid bringing new fleas back inside. It was literally impossible to enter or leave our building without being attacked by flea gangs hanging out on the lawn and shrubs near the door. I do believe they were all wearing tiny leather jackets and had nasty little tattoos.

(And I've got to tell you, just *writing* about all this, years later, I'm involuntarily scratching "phantom bites" on my ankles!)

I came up with a plan. I stocked up on aerosol cans of insect repellent, stuff that contained pesticides that are probably banned these days. The cans were parked just inside my apartment door. Just before I stepped outside—*every single time*—I'd spray my shoes, socks, pants, or bare legs if I happened to be wearing shorts. Then I'd race through the danger zone outside to minimize my exposure. Though this actually seemed to work, it's no way to live, folks.

But I couldn't spray Annie. It's one thing to spray poisons on my clothing, which would be laundered soon enough—or on my own legs, which also got thoroughly showered every day. But I didn't want to spray nasty stuff directly on Annie's fur and skin, from which she could have ingested it by licking her hands and feet.

The only way to keep her away from the fleas was to pick her up and carry her high as I charged out the door. I wouldn't put her down until we were well out into the parking lot. Fleas tend not to live on pavement. I would then walk her as far away from grass and foliage as possible. If she had to get within a yard of greenery, I'd pick her up and carry her again.

Prior to this, Annie had always gone to the bathroom on grass.

That had to change. She could have pooped on the street without much problem. But if she peed on the street, and the incline of the pavement was wrong, she'd end up with urine running onto her feet. Not desirable.

Then I came up with one of the few brilliant ideas of my life. There was a gravel parking lot a block away. The texture of the gravel and the fact that it wasn't a hard surface meant Annie could pee there and it would seep in rather than run off.

Theoretically.

It remained to be seen if she'd be willing to do what I had in mind. We walked to the gravel lot. And my little buddy peed and pooped there like she'd been doing it her whole life.

Problem solved. Eventually, the flea free-for-all passed.

Annie taught me...

If Hell exists, hosting and roasting sinners bound for eternal damnation, there are fleas there. Lots and lots of fleas.

Changes

Life without Hawkeye and Cindi sharing our apartment brought a whole series of changes for me and Annie. For one, Annie no longer spent her nights in the kitchen. She graduated to sleeping in my bedroom. I thought about buying her a little dog bed. As she often did, Annie made her own decision about where to sleep.

She chose to plop herself down on my laundry bag, which generally occupied a corner of the room beside my bed. Dogs naturally like the scent of their people. And, to be delicate about it, the laundry bag was *the* source of that scent.

And a pillow-case full of loose laundry offered another advantage: she could "nest" in it, using her little round hands to shape it to her preference. This skill for interior decorating comes to dogs instinctively. Wild canines commonly exhibit this behavior inside their dens and sleeping areas. And almost everyone who owns a dog tells stories about their pets *skritch-scratching* in the living room carpet before settling down for a nap.

Eventually, I went out and bought an actual hamper for dirty laundry, and Annie got a bed of her own. Two, actually. More on beds later.

Free at Last, Thank Dog Almighty, Free at Last!

"Help! My dog is tearing up my house and I'm ready to kill her!"

This is one of the most common complaints driving people to call a dog trainer. And the cause is almost always the same simple thing: people give their puppies and young dogs too much freedom much too soon.

There's no one best way to train the average dog (contrary to what many author-trainers may tell you in their books). But almost all trainers agree on this: puppies should *not* have free run of your home until they're *at least two years old*. The only sure-fire way to keep them from going to town on your couch cushions is to limit their access. How?

By using a crate to confine a younger puppy (especially one that isn't housebroken). And once a puppy has been reliably potty-trained to go outdoors only, then you can experiment with limited freedom by using baby gates to confine your teen-age puppy to a single small room—say, your kitchen.

Why is this important? Because even though dogs come close to being full-grown physically by their first birthday, emotionally and mentally they're still puppies for at least another year. So, even if you've diligently shaped your puppy's behavior for that first year, he's quite capable of forgetting everything he's learned when given an opportunity to get into trouble—with no one there to stop him.

It all comes down to impulse control. Teen-age dogs just haven't mellowed enough to resist temptation when they know there's no enforcer in sight.

I prefer to err even more to the side of caution. Annie was almost three by the time she forced the issue by moving heaven and earth (well, sixty pounds of dead weight, anyway) in order to get out of that kitchen. But confinement had served the intended purpose. By preventing her from partying in her formative years, she didn't develop bad habits—then or later.

This bears repeating: It's *much* easier to keep destructive habits from starting than it is to correct them *later*.

Part Two
MID-LIFE WONDERS

Hotels I: To Boldly Go Where
No Corgi Has Gone Before!

Another change in our lives: I began to take Annie on occasional overnight and weekend trips with me. By the time she was three, she'd demonstrated to me that her behavior was trustworthy. I had no doubts that I could even leave her alone in a hotel room, and she'd do no damage. She never let me down. If anything, the hotel should have paid her, since she searched so diligently for anything edible that the carpeting was invariably cleaner when we checked out than it had been when we arrived.

Annie had already proven herself to be a pleasant traveling companion on shorter jaunts close to home. When it was just the two of us in the car, she was content to ride down on the floor of the front passenger side. That way, I could keep an eye on her. She could see me. I could reach down and give her a little scratch now and then. And, if I had to make a short stop, she couldn't go flying very far and get hurt.

Annie's first long trip was south, to a *STAR TREK* convention outside of Baltimore.

A *STAR TREK* convention? Yes. I suppose my writing "claim to fame," such as it may be, is that I've written a number of *STAR TREK* stories over the years. In fact, my first-ever sale was a *STAR TREK* script, for the 1973-75 animated Saturday morning revival of the original Kirk-Spock-McCoy live-action *STAR TREK* series. In the years since, I've written a half-dozen best-selling *STAR TREK* novels, assorted articles about the ever-popular science fiction series, and sixty or so *STAR TREK* comic books for three different publishers. All of which made me a frequent guest-speaker at gatherings of STAR TREK fans in various parts of the country.

Soon after Cindi and Hawkeye left me and Annie on our own, I was invited to a rollicking Baltimore event known as Shore Leave. I checked with the hotel (Marriott's Hunt Valley Inn) and found that they allowed pets. So I decided to take Annie with me. If she enjoyed the trip, I'd bring her along on future journeys.

Annie slept on the floor most of the way down, listening to me singing along with tapes on the car stereo. As we drove south from New York, making our way through New Jersey and Delaware, I wondered how she'd react to a place as big and unfamiliar as a hotel, filled with strange people, sounds and smells. She'd always been friendly and receptive to new people and places. But this experience would be *new* on a grand scale.

I need not have worried.

True to form, Annie took everything in stride from the moment we arrived—quite literally. The first alien thing (so to speak) she encountered was the set of electric-eye doors at the hotel's front entrance. As we approached, I wondered if she'd be startled when the doors slid aside automatically. But when they opened, Annie marched straight on, as if she fully expected doors to open for her.

Once we got settled in our room, I took Annie on a tour of the convention areas. As we walked through the hotel, she tried to see and sniff everything within reach. If she'd had any qualms about being there, I'm sure they disappeared the first time we passed a room service tray left out on the corridor floor, complete with the remains of someone's meal. From Annie's point of view, this must have seemed like Paradise: any place where they put food on the floor was certainly fine with her.

The more time we spent among the STAR TREK fans attending the convention, the more Annie got greeted and petted and cooed at. As a "mini-celebrity," I normally got a pleasing but not intrusive share of attention from folks with kind words about my previous novels and questions about stories yet to come. I soon found much of that attention turned toward Annie.

People asked her name, wondered if it was okay to pet her, and shared stories about their own pets. A fair number asked if they could take Annie's picture—sometimes with me, and often without.

Annie continued to accompany me to STAR TREK and science fiction conventions for the rest of her life. My "official" photo for program booklets was a picture of the two of us—with Annie typically looking directly at the camera. She came onstage with me for almost all my talks. She greeted fans in hallways and ballrooms. She held hands with them, and posed for photos. One picture even appeared in *The Baltimore Sun*!

She also raised money for charity.

STAR TREK fans tend to be a good-hearted group, and conventions often feature fund raising activities for a variety of causes. At every Shore Leave weekend, there would be a charity auction. Once my closets had been picked clean of every auctionable piece of STAR TREK memorabilia I had to donate, we came up with a new idea: "*Ice Cream with Annie (& Howie)*" in return for a donation.

Annie's company and a cup of ice cream (purchased by me) went for surprising amounts of money. And even though she never got more than a finger-lick of ice cream herself, she was generally content with any activity that resulted her getting petted.

She did, however, draw the line at assaults on her dignity. The back story: one summer, I'd gone to one of the many Renaissance Fairs that take place around the country each year. In this case, it was the New York Renaissance Fair held in a lovely former arboretum north of New York City. I'm not big on souvenirs, but I found something irresistible—a set of cast resin "devil" horns on a string, worn atop the head with the string tied under the chin. And generally worn by people.

I bought them for Annie. I though it would be cute to put them on her for Halloween—or as a costume at our next STAR TREK convention.

When I brought them home, I got Annie to sit still while I tied the horns around her face. Then I stepped back. Took a look. And laughed. Annie's reaction was somewhat different, and her expression was pretty clear: "We are *not* amused!"

The next time we were at a convention, I tied the horns around her head just before leading her onstage. She gave me that look again, but gamely agreed to follow me out. She walked to center-stage and waited for a minute or so as the audience laughed and snapped flash-photos. Then, when she'd decided enough was enough, Annie shook her head to dislodge the horns, reached up with her hand, brushed them off her head, and marched off-stage to great applause (the little ham).

Less than pleased, Annie models her Halloween horns

Good dog that she was, she would have allowed me to inflict those horns on her again. But I never did.

Safety First

We were admittedly lucky Annie never got hurt riding unrestrained and loose in the car. It's much safer for pets to travel inside plastic airline-style crates, preferably secured by a seat-belt.

- ❀ For people who like their pets to ride on a seat so they can see out the windows, there are also a number of harnesses on the market. These interface with seat/shoulder-belt systems; they give pets some freedom of movement, yet still keep them safe in case of panic stop or accident.

- ❀ Never let dogs ride with their heads stuck out open car windows. They may like the feel of the breeze, but dirt and grit flying at high speed can injure dogs' eyes and ears.

- ❀ And never travel with your dog in the open bed of a pick-up truck!!

Annie taught me...

Think twice before risking the safety of a loved one—person or pet. There's no way to predict when your luck might run out. So don't take the chance. If we gamble, and lose, we have to live with the consequences.

Suitcases

Before I had Annie, I would not have believed the way dogs observe the world around them and their immediate home environment—and learn and remember every sound, sight, smell, association and activity that affects them. We've all heard stories about or directly experienced dogs responding to the jingle of keys, knowing this means there's a chance they might be going out for a walk or a ride.

Then there were suitcases. The first time a dog sees a suitcase, it means nothing. But the first time a dog sees a suitcase getting packed, and then sees a favorite human carrying that suitcase out the door and not coming back for days, well, *that's* a sequential experience that makes an impression.

After the first time, every time thereafter that Annie saw my suitcase come out of the closet, she would freak out. For one of two reasons: either she *wasn't* going with me, or she *was.*

If she *wasn't* going, then that was nothing short of cosmic tragedy and she'd act up a storm, making sure I understood fully the extent to which she felt abandoned, and eliciting maximum guilt. If she *was* going, then that was an adventure, and she couldn't wait until we actually got into the car and went.

In either case, from the moment the bag made its appearance, Annie wouldn't let me or it out of her sight. I guess she wanted to make sure I didn't forget her, and if I hadn't already planned to take her along, she'd make it her business to convince me otherwise.

Now, Annie actually had her own suitcase, a tote bag into which went her food, dish, snacks, comb and toys. Not quite the level of expeditionary provisions packed and carried seemingly everywhere by the parents of toddlers, but the idea is the same. Better to have what you need when you're away from home, and better to have it all in one bag.

Since Annie knew her bag didn't travel without her, I'd make sure to take hers out early in the process, to let her know she'd be going along. But I didn't pack her stuff until the very end, because as much as she fretted over seeing my things packed, the instant she saw hers getting packed, she positively exploded with excitement.

Annie really loved going wherever her people went. So do Mickey and Callie. And here's the worst-kept secret in the world: we hate to leave them behind as much as they hate being left.

Food IV:
Donut Doggie

Annie and I often had a human travelling companion for our STAR TREK convention trips to Maryland: Bob Greenberger. Bob has long worked in the science fiction and comic book fields, and was one of the best editors to ever work on the monthly STAR TREK comic book series.

Bob and I have been buddies for over twenty years. We originally met at a 1976 New York City STAR TREK convention, when I made my first appearance as a 22-year-old guest speaker and Bob was all of 17, working as a convention volunteer. We schmoozed, hung out, picked up girls (hey, we were young, male, and terribly innocent) and became fast friends.

Once Bob graduated from college and began his editorial work, and before he and his wife Debbie had kids, he and I would make the drive down on Friday afternoon. (Debbie would take the train from New York after work.)

By this time, Annie had already begun her career as a canine celebrity.

But she was willing to give up her usual travel space in the front-passenger-seat footwell so Bob could sit in the seat. This turned out to be not a huge sacrifice for Annie, since in trade she now had the entire back seat to herself, perched on pillows fit for a princess.

The drive from Long Island to Baltimore took roughly four hours, depending on traffic and the whims of what seemed to be perpetual construction along I-95. Plenty of time for me and Bob to gab and gossip, listen to tapes, and munch on a variety of snacks. It became customary for one of us to bring a box of golfball-sized donut "holes," which were sweet doughballs perfect for popping in your mouth. The joy of donuts, without the crumbs.

They came three-dozen to a cardboard container, as I recall. Whatever we didn't eat on the road would be snacked upon over the weekend. We drove with the box on the console between the front seats. The best traveling snacks are the kind you can locate and eat without too much fumbling or taking your eyes off the road. So these were pretty nearly perfect.

Though Annie could obviously sniff the sweet aroma of high-fat baked goods, she never made much of an effort to share them. She could have tried, by stepping up on the back of the console and reaching between the bucket seats. But she seemed to understand these weren't for her.

Or so I thought.

One trip, we arrived at the hotel, parked in the shaded drive at the main entrance, and left Annie in the car while we ran inside to check in and get our room keys.

We weren't gone for more than a few minutes. When we got back to the car, I found Annie sitting in the driver's seat—and let's just say the surplus supply of donut holes had been severely depleted. Subtracting what Bob and I had eaten from the original count, then surveying what was left, I figured Annie had gobbled a dozen or more—probably the equivalent of three or four *full-size* donuts. Given a little more time, you can bet she'd not only have devoured every single donut hole, she'd have licked the box clean of every last Corgi-cule.

I wanted to be mad at her, but how could I? She was a dog. Dogs are gluttons. And I had left her alone with temptation. I'd forgotten a basic principal of doggie behavior: if you don't want your dog to take advantage of a situation, don't give her the opportunity. In cases like these, an ounce of prevention is much better than several pounds of cure.

Besides, between the sheepish expression on Annie's face, and the powdered sugar on her nose, all I could do was laugh. And although her extra-full belly barely cleared the ground for the next day or so, I was thankful that her donut attack didn't make her sick.

Food V:
Edible Assets

And while we're talking about food again (most dogs' favorite topic): Can dogs *count*?

There's a famous tale about a circus horse named "Clever Hans." As part of his act, Hans would tap his hoof in response to his trainer telling him to count to a certain number. And Hans would get it right. Later, observers figured out that Hans was picking up unconscious non-verbal cues from the trainer or the people watching him. These cues would, in effect, signal him to stop "counting" when he reached the correct number. This sort of unintended response by a trained animal became known as the "*Clever Hans Syndrome*." And Hans was pretty clever, even if he couldn't actually count.

However, behaviorists have uncovered plenty of evidence that some animals can indeed judge relative amounts even if they can't do actual arithmetic. Although my own observations of Annie in action may have been somewhat unscientific, she convinced me that she could tell *more* from *less*, and make value judgments based upon such calculations.

Here's what we did:

Normally, if a small morsel of food—say, a single nugget of dry dog kibble—fell on the floor, Annie would scramble to grab it before anyone else could. It didn't matter if there was an entire bag of food on the kitchen counter; if there was a competing mouth in the vicinity (Hawkeye's mouth, for instance), Annie focused all her energy and skill on getting to that prize first. And she usually succeeded.

After Hawkeye moved away, I wondered if the loss of competition would affect her food-gathering behavior at all. Specifically, I wondered if she would pass up a single piece of food in order to get to a larger amount first, or if she would scarf up food based solely on the order in which she encountered it, regardless of the relative amounts involved.

To explore this question, I came up with an experiment. At mealtime, I'd let her follow me to the foyer of our apartment, where her food bag was stored on top of a cabinet (off the floor and out of her reach). She'd watch me scoop food from bag to bowl. Then I'd tell her to sit and stay in the foyer while I took her full bowl back into the kitchen, where she normally ate.

On the way, I'd take *one piece* of food and put it on the living room floor, midway between foyer and kitchen. I'd make sure Annie saw the lone piece on the floor. Then I'd remind her to "stay" as I continued into the kitchen and put her dish down in its usual spot. Finally, I'd release her with the word "Okay."

Every time we tried this, she'd race past the piece on the floor without grabbing it and rush straight into the kitchen to gobble up every last bit of her dinner. As soon as she'd emptied her bowl, she'd scamper back to the living room to eat the lone piece.

I think this behavior meant that Annie concluded that the single nugget on the floor would remain where it was, since there were no other dogs around (and I wasn't likely to eat it). So she decided it was preferable to go directly to the kitchen to eat what she knew to be a large quantity of food before returning to clean up the single piece.

And even if some other dog had beamed in and grabbed that one piece on the floor, hungry Annie would still have made the right choice in going for the larger amount first. *The Clever Annie Syndrome.*

Super-Model Annie

All dogs are beautiful, in their own individual ways. Even the homely, scruffy ones. But do all dogs have *camera sense*?

Annie sure did. In all her well-documented fifteen years, I hardly ever took or even saw a bad picture of her. In almost every photo, she's looking right at the camera, the canine embodiment of that uncommon presence known as "star quality."

Looking back on a lifetime of pictures, she plainly learned at an early age how to look a camera square in the eye. And I think I know the origin of this trait. Like many dogs, Annie basked in attention and praise. This is not inconsequential when it comes to a dog's trainability. Dogs who can take or leave praise may prove hard to motivate, and equally hard to reward with anything short of food. But lots of dogs, including Annie, are so attuned to the responses they get from people that they quickly learn how to elicit the responses they prefer.

Observant little dog that she was, I think Annie took early notice of the fact that sitting still for a picture earned her lots of praise and petting. Simple creatures that we humans are, that's apparently all it took to please us.

Even more interesting, Annie did not reserve this super-model's camera sense only for me. In our *STAR TREK* convention travels, fans would often stop us in and around the hotel and ask if they could take our picture.

Confession: *sometimes* they asked to take a picture of both of us. In which case, I would pick Annie up. And even while being held four feet off the ground, she'd hold still and smile. But often, I'd be asked, "Would *Annie* mind if I took her picture?"

No, of course she wouldn't. I got accustomed to this, and didn't take it personally. After all, of the two of us, Annie was far more cute and photogenic.

At subsequent conventions, some of the photographers would buttonhole me and show me the pictures taken the last time. And I always marveled at Annie's knack for gazing right into that lens, even if it happened to be pointed by a stranger.

On one of our Maryland visits, Bob Greenberger and I were doing a relaxed morning Q & A session in the main ballroom. Bob had his first-born baby Katie with him, and I, as usual, had Annie in the ballroom to meet and greet her public. Unknown to us, a photographer from *The Baltimore Sun* prowled the premises, snapping candids for the paper's Metro section.

A week or so later, I got an envelope from a Baltimore cousin, containing a surprise—a photo, clipped from the *Sun*, captured by that unnoticed hit-and-run camera. To see the picture is to see Annie's gift:

Bob sits crosslegged on the stage. He looks down at sleeping Katie cradled in his lap. He is *not* looking at the camera. Neither, obviously, is Katie. I sit on the stage steps. I am caught in mid-gesture. I look like a dork. I am also *not* looking at the camera.

Annie, bless her little photogenic heart, is the *only* one with her eye on the camera, offering her most affable smile.

Star quality all the way.

Hotels II:
Run For Daylight

As I've said, Annie was polite and well-trained—but not perfect on either score. One time, her own imperfection—and my own carelessness—nearly resulted in disaster.

It was another arrival at another *STAR TREK* convention at the Hunt Valley Inn. Following the famous donut-hole incident, I brought Annie to the front desk with me as I checked in. Then, key in hand, we found our room, which was on the ground floor, down a hallway that was essentially a straight shot from the lobby. Per routine, I was about to leave Annie in the room while I went back to the car to bring our baggage in.

As at many hotels, the doors to the Hunt Valley Inn guest rooms close by themselves. Slowly. When I returned with a load of luggage, I entered the room as the door eased shut behind me. Slowly.

Slowly enough for leashless Annie to dart out and take off down the corridor. I dropped everything and charged out after her.

Don't let those short legs fool you: Corgis can *run*!

I shouted for her to stop and come back. She ignored me. I ran after her—which is exactly the opposite of what every trainer (including me) says you should do when your dog is running away from you. Pursue a runaway, and you're doing exactly what your dog wants: playing the "*Chase Me!*" game.

But, faced with a crisis of my own making, I wasn't thinking like a trainer. I was thinking like a terrified dog-lover, my mind overwhelmed by the image of Annie racing right out those self-opening doors, into the parking lot—and getting creamed by a car.

Merrily galloping as fast as her little legs could go, Annie blew past the elevators. Past the doors leading out to the pool. Past the gift shop. Hell, she even passed by the coffee shop—and you know how much she liked food! I kept chasing and calling her. She kept ignoring me. Finally, in desperation, I roared out her name in the loudest and angriest voice of my life. She stopped in her tracks, just short of the lobby. And I scooped her up before she could get going again.

I was furious with her (even though the whole incident was my fault). And I was as relieved as I've ever been that she'd allowed me to catch her. So I hugged her and scolded her as we went back to our room, and I swore I'd never be that careless again.

Hotels III:
Annie the Brave

Yeah, yeah, I swore I'd never let Annie run out of a hotel room like that again. And I never did. I also wanted to make certain that some unsuspecting hotel housekeeper wouldn't inadvertently give her a chance to escape. Upon arrival at any hotel, it became my custom to routinely inform housekeeping that I had a small dog staying with me, and I wouldn't need my room cleaned until I checked out. To make sure this message got to the staff members who actually went to clean the rooms, I would post a note on my door.

I thought I had all bases covered. I was wrong.

On one stay at a high-rise hotel in Scranton, Pennsylvania, I took all my precautions and then went out to dinner. When I returned to my room, I saw that—*uh-oh!*—my door was open. Did I fear the worst? You bet I did! Instead, I was totally unprepared for what I found, which was —

— a pair of hotel maintenance workers, just inside my doorway. They were held at bay by my little Corgi, who stood three or four paces further inside the room, barking ferociously and protecting our temporary territory. The maintenance guys had come to check on a broken television, but they'd come to the wrong room—in more ways than one: not only was my TV working fine, but Annie wouldn't even let them in. They weren't sure whether to laugh at this pint-sized guard dog or to be respectful of flashing teeth. Wisely, they opted to avoid confrontation.

When they left in search of the mysterious malfunctioning set, I picked Annie up and told her what a good girl she'd been, and how happy I was that she'd chosen responsibility over another run for freedom.

Hotels IV:
Beds

When you have pets that shed, animal hair is something you just have to live with. No amount of grooming or vacuuming can eliminate the stuff. We've all been to homes where pets were permitted to sack out on couches, beds or chairs, whatever their preference.

But I wanted my visitors to be able to sit on our couches without ending up covered in dog hair. And I wanted to be able to sleep in my own bed without getting a mouthful of fur.

So Annie had been trained to stay off people furniture. And she was generally pretty good about it. In fact, considering her stature, I didn't even think she could get up on a bed. This was just another example of my underestimating Annie's determination—not to mention her apparent ability to leap tall beds in a single bound.

I first discovered the truth during one of our hotel stays. When I returned to the room, I found some telltale cream-colored hairs amid the slight wrinkles at the center of the bedspread. I may not have known it before, but Annie had obviously figured out how to levitate onto the king-sized bed that was twice her height. And that's where she'd napped—until she heard the metal key turning in the door lock.

Years later, age and technology caught up with her. As she got older, her hearing wasn't as sharp as it had been. Plus, hotels had changed from old-fashioned metal keys to electronic card-keys. The new-fangled locks operated almost silently, and I was able to creep into the room to find her sleeping soundly at the heart of the mattress.

I would have let her stay there. By that time of her life, she'd certainly earned the right to extra comfort (on the road, at least). But as soon as she woke up, she promptly (though sheepishly) jumped off the bed, where she knew she wasn't allowed.

From then on, we expected her to grab an occasional nap on a nice hotel bed. But she never tried to bend that rule at home.

Well… almost never. But that's another story.

Hotels V:
Sleeping, on Guard

Annie was so well-behaved and trustworthy by the time we started going on road-trips together that I never felt the need for a travel crate. In retrospect, this was dumb on my part. And I heartily recommend to anyone traveling with a dog: *take a crate.*

For one thing, having your dog ride in the crate in the car is much safer than the way I travelled with Annie. And when you reach your destination, you'll have a safe, familiar place to keep your dog when you have to leave her behind in your hotel room. So you won't have to worry about your pup bolting if a hotel employee happens to open the door to your room when you're not there.

Since I'd raised Annie before the days when crate-training at home became fashionable, I didn't even consider getting one for travel. Had I brought one along, Annie would have slept in her own little "room-within-in-a-room." Instead, I always brought her pillow-bed along with us. The problem was, finding the right place for the bed. The first time I did this, I just put her bed in a corner.

· But Annie had a different preference. And as usual, she expressed it clearly. I noticed that she liked sleeping in the closet, and since I knew how she thought, I immediately knew why.

First, recall that dogs are den animals. In a strange place, Annie naturally chose the only enclosed, dark space.

Then, in most hotel rooms, the closet is just inside the room door. So, by sleeping in the closet, Annie could guard the room entrance like Cerberus, guardian of Hades in Greek mythology. (Okay, yeah, Cerberus was a dog with a few extra heads. But Annie could *eat* like a dog with a few extra heads.)

She also knew that I never left the room without my shoes, which I usually put on the closet floor when I wasn't wearing them. If she slept on top of my shoes, she could keep track of my comings and goings.

So, for Annie, sleeping in hotel-room closets was the perfect choice, letting her feel safe and secure. Pretty smart dog.

Furniture (Over...)

Although Annie generally abided by the rules and stayed off furniture, she did have her *Sofa Rebellion*.

That historic event occurred during one of our periodic roommate switcheroos. After Cindi had moved to the West Coast, a co-worker and friend of hers named Robert had moved in to take over the empty bedroom. Robert was a nice guy, and Annie liked him. He lived with us for a couple of years, and we fell into a routine whenever we'd watch television in the living room.

We had a big country-style sofa and loveseat combo, arranged in an L-shape. I usually reclined on the loveseat with my feet propped on the padded arm. From that position, with a couple of pillows under my head, I could do two vital things: see the TV screen, and reach down to pet Annie lying on the carpet next to the loveseat. Robert, who was much taller than I am, would stretch out on the larger sofa.

Eventually, Robert changed jobs, and moved out to shorten his marathon commute. By now, Annie knew the signs: boxes and packing meant an imminent personnel shuffle in our pack. In this case, no one moved in to replace Robert.

So Annie declared dibs on the sofa.

I discovered this by accident. Not long after Robert left, I came home from work to find an inordinate amount of Annie hair on the big couch. Plainly, while I was out, she'd climbed up and spent part of her day (or most of it, for all I could tell) napping in the corner of what she now regarded as *her couch*.

This presented a training problem. There wasn't much I could do to keep her off if I wasn't home to catch her in the act.

Later on, I learned all sorts of techniques that might have worked to keep a dog off furniture in the owner's absence. But at the time, Annie had me at a nearly-complete disadvantage. In fact, I was ready to give up.

About the only lame countermeasure I came up with was to throw some old sheets on the couch to at least keep it from becoming covered with dog hair. Then I had a **Eureka**! moment: she liked being on the couch because it was a soft place to sleep. So I tipped the seat cushions up, which left her a not-so-soft vinyl-covered under-cushion.

I did that for a couple of weeks. Annie never went up on the under-cushions. Then I put the soft cushions back down, and looked for signs of dog hair upon returning home after work. No dog hair. Apparently, my last-ditch strategy was enough of a deterrent that it convinced Annie not to bother trying any more.

The way I see it, she let me win one. And it was about time!

Annie taught me...

It may not be easy to outsmart a worthy adversary. But don't give up too quickly: the next thing you try may do the trick.

...And Furniture (Under)

Annie actually preferred to be *under* furniture rather than *on* it. There's an easy explanation for this: dogs are den animals. Most wild canines have historically spent at least some of their time in underground burrows. And we're not talking caves here. We're talking spaces barely big enough to crawl into.

Which is one reason why crate-training is generally recognized as the best way to housebreak puppies. Where people go wrong is looking at the crate from a *human* point of view. I've lost count of how many of my dog-training clients buy crates *much* too big for their teeny puppies. They think: "Gee, if I were in there, I'd sure want it to be roomy." But we humans live in *houses*, not *dens*.

Given a small "den," a dog thinks: "Gee, this is barely big enough for me to stand up straight. Just barely big enough to turn around in, if I squeeze. Barely big enough to sleep in, if I curl up. Hey, I *love* this place!"

So, wherever Annie lived, she picked out her favorite small spaces. That loveseat upon which I used to stretch out and watch TV had just enough room for her to squeeze under it, if she crawled on her belly.

Years later, when my wife Susan and I bought our house, we also went out and got some new furniture. That old workhorse loveseat ended up retired to the basement and we shopped for a new full-size couch. Most people make such purchase decisions based on style, upholstery choices and price. We had another factor to consider. And, quite honestly, it was the most important one: whatever we

Annie peeks out from her under-sofa "den"

picked *had* to have room for Annie (and future Corgis) to squeeze under the thing.

Lots of people take measurements to see if prospective furniture will fit into their homes. We may be the only people on the planet who measured a couch's ground clearance to make sure our dog would fit *under* it!

If you think this was simply a quirk of Annie's, I assure you our two current Corgis, Mickey and Callie, both love to hide out under that very same couch.

Annie also liked to be under our bed. Now, she did have her own bed, in a nice denlike corner of our bedroom, underneath a vanity counter. And that's where she'd go to sleep when the lights went out. But somewhere around dawn, she'd leave her bed and crawl under ours. Why?

Well, I always got up first. And positioned as she was under my side of the bed, Annie could detect the slightest motion—motion that might mean I was getting out of bed.

And each time I'd move, Annie would pop out from underneath, full of expectation. (We called those explosive exits "Annie Eruptions.") If I failed to

The Long Arm of the Law (in Absentia)

Lots of otherwise good dogs give in to the temptation of that nice soft sofa or recliner when we're not home to discourage them. But there are some effective ways to make corrections and enforce the law when we're absent:

🐾 Place upside-down mousetraps on the couch. When your unsuspecting pooch tries to sneak up there, the traps snap and scare the hell out of her. This may dissuade her from trying again.

🐾 Put a sheet of aluminum foil on the couch. Many dogs don't like the feel of the stuff, or the metallic rattling sound it makes. (Wrapping aluminum foil around unauthorized chewing targets, such as chairlegs or books on low shelves, may solve that problem as well.)

🐾 Use one of several inexpensive mats on the market, some of which issue a slight electrical shock when touched (similar to the static-electricity shocks we get from doorknobs on dry winter days). Other mats emit an annoying sound when a pet lands on them. These work because they provide consistent negative reinforcement even when we're gone.

get out of bed, she'd crawl right back under. And she'd do this over and over until I'd finally get the message: "Hurry up and *FEEEEED* me!"

Separation Anxieties

There were some trips when I couldn't take my dog along. Back when Cindi and I shared custody of Annie and Hawkeye, if one of us had to go away, we knew both puppies were in the safe care of the "parent" who stayed behind. And long before I ever took Annie on the road with me, there were occasions where Cindi and I went on the same trip.

The first time that happened, during a damp and chilly weekend in late winter, we found a boarding kennel not far from where we lived. When we came back and retrieved our dogs, we were extremely unhappy with what we found: two cold wet dogs who'd been left in outdoor kennel runs obviously open to the elements. On top of that, both came home with minor cases of kennel cough.

That was the first and last time we used a boarding kennel. (Which isn't to say there aren't *any* good boarding kennels. To the contrary: there are many. So how do you find one? Ask for recommendations from people you trust; and check out any potential kennels in person before you leave your beloved pet with them.)

Next time we had to travel without the dogs, Cindi arranged for us to leave them at Hawkeye's breeder, a nice lady named Jane who boarded dogs only as occasional favors for people she knew. Annie and Hawkeye shared a kennel run so they wouldn't be lonely. They were able to play and sleep together just as they did at home.

Jane also had an indoor kennel shed in case of bad weather. And when we drove over to pick them up after we returned, we found two happy, healthy dogs acting very much like kids who didn't really want summer camp to end.

After Cindi and Hawkeye moved west, Jane was nice enough to host Annie on the next occasion when I had to leave her behind.

I really hated to go away without her. I worried about her. And I missed her. Most people who've had dogs know the feelings. But at least I knew she'd be safe and reasonably happy staying at Jane's.

As soon as I got home, I went to retrieve Annie—and I was somewhat surprised to find her happily running around (and running) Jane's house. It seemed that shortly after my departure, Annie had gone into her Houdini act, escaped from her kennel run and raced around Jane's spacious yard, daring the world to try and catch her.

Fortunately, the yard was securely fenced, and Annie was eventually apprehended. After that, she was invited into Jane's house to spend her stay as one of the family—in part, because Jane truly appreciated Annie and thought she was both smart and cute.

Unfortunately, we soon lost Jane as a dogsitter when her husband became seriously ill. Caring for him took much of her time and energy, and she not only could no longer board other people's dogs; she also had to find foster homes for many of her own fine Collies.

Stay-at-Home Annie

So: I'd ruled out boarding kennels. And we'd lost Annie's "Camp Jane." I needed a new solution to the problem almost all dog-owners eventually face: what to do with your furry friend when you have to leave home without her. When roommate Robert shared our apartment, he graciously agreed to look after Annie when I went away for an occasional weekend.

That was an ideal solution. She'd be left in familiar surroundings with a person whom she knew and liked, and who knew many of her habits and quirks. He also happened to be a trustworthy guy.

After Robert moved out, I couldn't find anyone I knew who needed a place to live, and I really didn't care to invite a total stranger into my apartment, humble though it may have been. So Annie and I went solo for a couple of years. It was actually kind of nice for us to have the place to ourselves for a change.

Solitude doesn't have to be lonely, and it wasn't, as long as I had Annie with me.

But solitude did mean I had no live-in dog-sitter. So I had to come up with an alternative that was comfortable for both me and Annie.

By that time, I'd become friendly with neighbors both across the hall and upstairs. And they both offered to look after Annie when needed. Upstairs neighbor Millie was a friendly middle-aged woman, divorced, living alone. She welcomed the company—and she loved spoiling Annie. Which was fine with Annie.

Across the hall, single mom Emily lived with her 10-year-old daughter Maggie, a bright friendly kid who loved animals. Petless themselves, Emily and Maggie took quite a liking to Annie, and she was always welcome in their apartment. To be accurate, Annie *made* herself welcome there. How?

Simple. My door and theirs were literally opposite each other, separated only by our six-foot-wide hallway. When both doors happened to be open at the same time, Annie made it her custom to march right into their apartment for a visit.

The first time I asked Emily to look after Annie, the plan was that Annie would simply stay in my apartment. Emily and Maggie would come over to feed her and take her out for walks. If they wanted to play with her, they were more than welcome to stay with Annie as often or as long as they chose, and equally welcome to spend time at my place watching cable TV (which they didn't have). As it turned out, they invited Annie into their apartment and she ended up spending the weekend with them.

I offered to pay them for taking care of Annie, but Emily had a better idea. Since her daughter really wanted a dog of her own, if I had no objection, Maggie would be primarily responsible for Annie's upkeep (under her mom's supervision). And I agreed to pay Maggie five dollars a day.

This worked out well all around: I knew Annie would be in good and loving hands; she wouldn't be lonely without me; Maggie got a "loaner" dog and a paying job; and we helped Emily teach her daughter responsibility.

It always made me happy to know Annie was welcome at other people's homes. Dogs should be welcome wherever their human companions go—but only if they (the dogs) are taught to behave well enough to warrant that kind of welcome. Through a happy combination of Annie's personality and intelligence, and the training she had as a puppy, she usually got the hospitality she deserved.

One weekend, I was summoned to do best-man duties at my friend Joel Davis's wedding in Rhode Island. I'd only be away overnight.

On this occasion, Annie was recruited by yet another set of friends who had known her most of her life: my STAR TREK travelling companion Bob Greenberger and his wife Debbie.

Bob and Debbie had been thinking about adding a puppy to their household. So they thought that hosting Annie for a couple of days would give them a taste of what it would be like to have their own dog.

My only concern was how Annie would behave around Bob and Debbie's six-month-old baby Katie. Annie was about five years old herself at the time. She'd never had a problem with toddlers and children, and she'd grown up knowing my niece Kimberly, who was a one-and-half-year-old mini-person at the time Annie came to live with me. But, to be honest, Annie hadn't really had much exposure to little babies. And it's not uncommon for dogs to get spooked by the unpredictable motions and noises made by babies.

So we did a test run.

The weekend before I was to go away, I brought Annie over to the Greenbergers' house. I wanted to reacquaint her with Bob and Debbie, let her familiarize herself with their home, and introduce her to baby Katie. If Annie showed the slightest negative reaction to Katie, I'd make other arrangements for her care in my absence.

When we arrived, I put some of Annie's chew toys on the floor, and let her roam around Bob and Debbie's house. New surroundings rarely phased her, and this time was no different. She explored, as always, and in that way made a new place her own. Then came the true test.

With Annie back on-leash, we put Katie on the floor. And we watched as baby and dog inspected each other. Katie seemed fine with Annie, and vice versa. Then came a crucial potential conflict. Katie picked up a rawhide toy and offered it to Annie.

Some dogs are very protective of such items as favorite toys and food bowls. Such surly possessiveness is something young puppies should be taught not to exhibit. Without meaning any harm, they can get grabby. And that's when an unsuspecting child can end up getting nicked by a tooth.

Annie and Katie Greenberger enjoy their summit meeting

The chew-toy Katie held in her little fist was one of those rolled rawhide things, knotted at each end, and hardened to form something shaped roughly like a bone. It was about four inches, end to end. And Katie gripped it at dead-center, which didn't give Annie much of a safety margin. I held her leash, ready to stop her if it looked like her teeth were on a collision course with Katie's fingers.

Generally speaking, Annie *loves* rawhide. And at home, she was none too shy about grabbing toys from adult hands with great gusto. But Annie seemed to know this toy was being offered by a baby. Frontal assaults simply would not do here. Instead of reacting with an eager lunge, she waited and sized up the situation.

Then she cautiously reached *around* Katie's hand. Barely opening her mouth, Annie used only her little front teeth to grip the knob at one end of the toy. And she didn't pull. She waited to see if Katie would release the toy, or hold onto it.

Now it was up to Katie. Most toddlers in this situation will respond by pulling back on the toy, which is what you don't want them to do. Impromptu tug-of-war games can easily escalate, spin out of control, and end with an accidental bite.

Just as Annie had approached the situation with composure, so (amazingly) did little Katie. When Annie gently tugged on the toy, Katie let it go. Both had passed this test with flying colors, and Katie's parents and I were certain Annie's stay would go smoothly.

As a matter of fact, Annie proved a pleasant and trouble-free little houseguest. When I returned from Rhode Island to pick her up, Bob and Debbie reported there'd only been one casualty: a *muffin* Debbie had brought home from work, wrapped in a paper sack and buried in her tote bag.

(By now, you probably know Annie well enough to see where this is going.)

At some point over the weekend, Debbie remembered the muffin and went to retrieve it from the tote bag. The bag was still on the floor near the front door where she'd left it Friday evening. Instead of the leftover muffin, however, she found only a slightly tattered paper bag and a few crumbs. Annie had long since homed in on the edible stowaway and dispatched it with her usual attention to neatness and precision. And Debbie realized she was hosting not a mere dog but a furry food-seeking missile.

Annie taught me...

It's always good to come home after a trip.
Even better: when your dog is there to welcome you.
No one greets you like your dog does.
Best of all: taking your dog with you.

Annie & Kids

Her summit meeting with little Katie Greenberger was typical of Annie's behavior around children, especially small ones. The affection was generally mutual, maybe because Corgis don't get very large themselves, and the more petite ones (like Annie) always look like puppies. So they're not very threatening to toddlers.

It also doesn't hurt that Corgis are so darned cute that they resemble live stuffed animals. I still laugh over the time that Susan and I were walking Annie's successors, Mickey and Callie, and a little girl across the street called out: "Look! *Bunny dogs!*" Even children who are wary of other dogs, especially larger animals, tend to light up at the sight of a Corgi.

For her part, Annie always seemed to have an innate understanding that tiny humans were fragile and needed to be watched over. Annie and my niece Kimberly always enjoyed seeing each other. Since Annie was the only dog in our family, she dedicated herself to the task of making sure Kim learned how to behave around dogs. Kim always wanted to pet her, and Annie always obliged. Sometimes, when Annie kissed her too enthusiastically, Kim would scrunch up her face and declare, "No yickks!" But she was always laughing when she said it.

Later, when she was about three, Kim would grab Annie's leash and insist on holding it while we walked. Now, as gentle and small as Annie was, she was more than strong enough to knock over a three-year-old. So we evolved a system where Kimberly would clutch the looped end of the leash in her hands, and I would hold the middle. This allowed Kim to feel like she was actually walking Uncle Howard's doggie, and let me serve as a buffer to absorb any unexpected pulling—from either end of the leash.

By the time Annie was well into middle age, I noticed another interesting behavior, probably prompted by both her vigilant solicitude toward children and her natural herding instincts. Whenever we found ourselves walking with a friend or neighbor pushing a baby in a stroller, Annie always kept up a guardian's pace, marching with her nose just ahead of the leading wheel as if to head off any trouble ahead.

Apartment Wars

After a couple of years without a roommate, an unfortunate situation arose that forced Annie and me to leave the apartment where I'd been living for ten years, and where she'd lived her whole life.

I hadn't been planning to leave, but the apartment complex had recently been bought by new owners—businessmen with grandiose ideas. They decided it was time for dowdy, timeworn Westbury Garden Apartments to morph into overpriced condominiums.

"Going condo" meant old residents (or new ones) would buy their apartments and pay monthly maintenance fees roughly equal to the national budget of France. What it really meant, potentially, was plenty o' profit for the investors who owned the overall property.

What does this have to do with dogs? Give me a minute. I'll get to it. Now, back to our sordid tale of real-estate rackets...

New York State and Nassau County had reasonable laws on the books, protecting rental tenants from being thrown out if they either didn't want to or couldn't afford to buy their apartments. Still, from a management point of view, condos work best when most if not all the apartments are purchased rather than rented.

And there was one main obstacle in the way of the grand nefarious plan to turn our dowdy apartments into luxury condos.

By law, a rental apartment complex could not go condo without the majority-vote approval of current tenants. Apartments that were empty at the time of such a vote apparently counted in the property owners' favor. I guess the theory was, "If they ain't a'gin' you, they're for you."

So it became the apparent goal of the new owners to legally empty out as many apartments as they could before the Big Vote.

One way to do that: raise rents to unaffordable levels, and in that way, force renters out. That can take some time, however, since the property owners and their investors would then have to wait until leases expired.

Another method, with quicker results: have the management's law firm send scary letters to tenants with dogs, informing said tenants that they had *two weeks* in which to get rid of their pets or vacate the premises. Essentially, they were evicting people who had dogs.

I, of course, was one such tenant. But their letter didn't scare me. It made me furious!

Could they do this? Plainly, it wasn't right, and it certainly *shouldn't* be legal. But I didn't know for sure. I was determined to find out—and in a hurry.

First, a little background. When I had moved in almost ten years earlier, the standard leases technically stated *No Dogs Allowed*. But I noticed this was not enforced. Several tenants had dogs, and walked them openly. And even one of the live-in superintendents had a dog.

Before Cindi and I got Hawkeye and Annie, we asked the nice lady in the rental office if this would cause any problems. By then, I'd been an exemplary tenant for a few years, and Sonia the office lady liked me. If our dogs behaved, there'd be no objections. For the next half-dozen years, my lease was renewed without question. I always paid my rent on time, and made sure my dog was never a nuisance of any kind. So here I am, minding my own business, and the lousy creeps are trying to *evict* me?!?

They picked the wrong victim.

Let's be clear about something: I'm not a lawyer. Never went to law school. Didn't want to pay a lawyer if I could help it. Ahhh, *but* I did watch the excellent network (and later cable-TV) drama series *THE PAPER CHASE*, about a group of Harvard law students and their eminent and majestic contracts-law mentor, Professor Charles W. Kingsfield.

Contracts law! I loved that show, and the legalities of contracts were what I needed to know about. I recalled that Professor Kingsfield always seemed to be teaching about the elegance and logic inherent in a proper contract.

So I decided to *pretend* that I'd consulted with an eminent and name-less contracts-law expert. Nobody had to know it was the fictional Professor Kingsfield.

Herewith (lawyers are always using words like *herewith*) I share with you my logical approach to this legal dilemma:

1. I had signed a lease.
2. Leases are binding, as long as the conditions contained therein are are followed by both parties.
3. At the time I signed the lease, I had a dog.
4. The apartment management *knew* I had a dog. Therefore, their approval of the lease amounted to *de facto* permission that I could continue to live there with my dog.
5. And they had no legal right to alter that lease in mid-stream.

When I consulted with the local consumer protection office, they con-firmed that I was on solid legal ground. Next, I did something the result of which will always give me great pleasure: I *bluffed* the attorneys!

What's more, it *worked*!

Sort of.

I wrote a very officially-worded letter to the management attorneys assigned the task of scaring the stuffing out of apartment tenants. (Is there a special law-school class that teaches them how to do that?) I told them I had consulted with a friend who was an expert in contracts law—and who would be willing to represent me *without charge* should it be necessary to go to court (forgive me, Professor Kingsfield). I presented the above case, and waited for a reply. In surprisingly short order, I got one.

A somewhat chagrined attor-ney called me. Without admit-ting that I would win this case, he tried to make a deal. Now, admittedly, they did have one inescapable fact on their side: my lease would be up in a few months, and I knew they did have the right to offer me a

Disposable Dogs

An astonishing number of dogs dumped at animal shelters seem to be there for the lamest of reasons:

* people suddenly develop allergies
* they get divorced
* they move
* they don't have the time for a pet

I don't mean to be judgmental (well, sure I do; a little, at least). Sometimes life does indeed throw a curve that forces people to part with their pets. But too many people just seem to take the easy way out, with little or no thought to how their animals will feel when they're abandoned.

renewal that specifically excluded dogs. So, since I obviously was not parting with Annie, the best I could get was a stand-off.

While they couldn't throw me out until my then-current lease expired, I would have little choice but to move out at that point.

Since they *wanted* me to move out (remember, their goal was to empty out apartments and get rid of tenants who might possibly vote *against* the new condominium plan), they "graciously" offered to let me out of my lease any gosh-darned time I wanted, prior to the actual expiration date. Wasn't that *nice* of them?

Well, I got the best deal I could. And, come summer, I lined up a new roommate and started looking for a new home.

Annie taught me...

Loyalty.
Nothing could come between me and
my dogs. I'd live out of my car before
I'd give them up!

The Road to Flower Street

My next roommate was to be Lynne Stephens, a bright young friend who had just finished grad school at Syracuse University, and had a job lined up with the Lifetime cable television network in New York City. Since Lynne was spending her summer working in England, it was up to me to find us all a decent place to live.

Finding an apartment if you have a dog is not an easy task. Many landlords and management companies have a blanket pooch prohibition. It's not fair, but I understand: To be blunt, many dog-owners are inconsiderate pigs.

However, let's not forget that many *non*-dog-owners are *also* inconsiderate pigs.

The ugly truth is that many people with dogs (and cats, too) allow their pets to defecate and urinate indoors, and otherwise generally trash their apartments. The resultant damage incurs extra maintenance expenses for people and companies who own apartments. So I can't completely blame them for their prejudice against pet-owners.

What I *can* blame them for is lumping all of us together. If you've read this far, you know how I feel on this subject: there's *no excuse* for pets not being properly trained and restrained from destructive behavior. And many of us do train our pets. We who do are more than willing to vouch for our pets—I have no objection at all to rental policies requiring an extra damage deposit for pet owners. This deposit should be *fully-refundable* if there's no pet-related damage when an apartment is vacated.

Apartment complexes on Long Island had a nearly universal ban on dogs. So I had to look for whole houses, two-family houses, or homes that had been legally subdivided into two or more apartment units. I toted pictures of Annie around with me so prospective landlords and rental agents could see what kind of dog she was. One picture showed her with my niece Kim, to clearly show Annie's pint-size in comparison to a seven-year-old kid.

I also sought to pre-empt objections to a pet by *offering* a refundable damage deposit, in addition to the standard security deposit. That seemed the best way to demonstrate my confidence that my well-mannered little dog wouldn't do any damage, no matter where we lived. I was also more than willing to bring Annie to be "interviewed," if that was what it took to secure a decent place to live.

Finally, after weeks of searching, I found a nice split-level house for rent at a reasonable cost. The absentee landlord was a middle-aged Portuguese gentleman named Antonio, who'd done well enough since coming to America to purchase this home as a rental investment. In a gallant gesture that harkened back to old-world ways and simpler times, he considered my handshake sufficient assurance, and saw no need for an extra deposit against pet damage.

His wife wasn't so sure, but I was determined to be worthy of Antonio's confidence. So Annie and I moved into our new home, complete with a fenced-in yard for off-leash romping, something Annie had rarely been able to do in her life.

After a decade in an apartment, with its thin walls and ceiling, I have to admit it was a welcome relief to be back in a single-family house, not unlike the one in which I'd grown up. We had a neighborhood with lots of tree-lined streets for our daily walks. It was typical suburbia, and it felt like home.

When Lynne moved in after returning from London, our little makeshift family-unit was complete. By then, I'd quit my public-information-writing job at the American Diabetes Association in Manhattan. After some success with part-time freelance writing, I'd decided to try self-employment full-time. That meant I got to be home with Annie all the time, which was fine with both of us. She had just turned seven, well into doggie middle-age. We'd become so bonded that we were almost a single entity. The more time we got to spend together, the better.

Health-Care Scare

For many small and medium-size dogs, life spans of twelve to sixteen years aren't uncommon. Dogs don't get colds or the flu, and seem to become ill much less frequently than we do. If a dog is well-supervised, serious injuries are also rare. With proper care, a bit of luck, and the blessing of good genes, many dogs age much more gracefully than their human companions.

This was true of Annie. The most noticeable change, as she advanced into her middle years, was that she spent more time napping. But when she was up, she was still full of energy and puppy joy, always ready to play. I was lulled into the expectation that she was unstoppable —

— until the morning she literally dragged herself out of bed, and seemed unable to descend the half-flight of carpeted steps leading from the bedrooms to the rest of our rented split-level. At first, I just thought she was a little stiff from her night's sleep. When I went down to the kitchen to make my breakfast and serve her regular morning dog biscuit, I expected her to follow as she always did.

But I found her at the top of the stairs, unwilling or unable to come down. It was a simple fact that Annie normally did not hesitate for even a millisecond where food was involved. For her to stay at the top of those steps meant she had to be hurting. And I immediately thought the worst (a trait I inherited from my mother).

When I was a kid, there'd been a nearby house with a red dachshund, paralyzed from the shoulders back. He got around with the aid of a little cart under his belly, the wheels substituting for his hind legs. I'd always heard that long-backed dogs (like Welsh Corgis) were more susceptible to disk and spine injuries, especially if they were allowed to become overweight. I don't know if medical facts back up that truism, but that's what I thought about as I drove Annie to our wonderful vet's office for an emergency examination.

From the time I met him at Annie's first puppy check-up, Dr. Arthur Wilder at Westbury Animal Hospital reminded me of Muppets creator Jim Henson. Both men had bushy beards and a gentle, reassuring manner. I'd liked Dr. Wilder instantly and always felt Annie was in the best of hands when the hands were his.

This time, I needed as much reassurance as I could get. First, Dr. Wilder examined Annie's back manually, confirming that she was in some pain. Then a set of X-rays were taken, which showed...nothing. This was good news. There were no signs of degenerative disk disease, arthritis or any other obvious damage.

Dr. Wilder explained that middle-aged dogs, like people, might occasionally sleep at an odd angle, or simply bend or move in the wrong way. The result (familiar to many of us humans) can be pain ranging from a dull ache to incapacitating agony. In all likelihood, that was what had happened to Annie. The prescription was simple: some initial medication to ease the pain, followed by reduced activity.

With dogs, oddly enough, it's sometimes better to let them feel their pain, if it's not too excruciating. The discomfort is what tells them to take it easy and let their bodies heal naturally. So, for a few days, Annie rested. Then, as dogs will do, she made it clear by how she moved that she felt better. Even though she'd rebounded quickly, I took this as a warning of things to come.

Annie's weight had crept higher as she'd aged and become less active. Depending on their bone structure, female Corgis may weigh up to 28 pounds. But Annie was small for the breed, and her adult weight had stabilized for several years at an optimal 22 pounds. Then, almost unnoticed, she'd added a few ounces at a time, to reach a high of 25 pounds.

She wasn't really fat, and it was only when I compared side-by-side photos of her at age three with more current pictures that I could see a clear difference. Let's call her "bulky."

Even though the extra three pounds probably had nothing to do with her temporary back problem, this was a trend worth reversing.

We've all seen fat old dogs who had trouble moving, much less running. I didn't want Annie to end up that way.

To combat middle-aged spread, we changed our walking habits. Instead of taking her out merely to go to the bathroom, our walks became longer, at a pace geared for exercise. One of the nice things about walking a short dog is, those little legs have to move fast to keep up with a brisk human stride.

And we went out three times a day, every day, when the weather cooperated. During the hottest part of summer, we'd skip our walk under the noon-day sun, since she was not a mad dog and I was not an Englishman. But even in July and August, we'd be out there striding around the block in the cooler air of early mornings and late evenings. In winter, only the worst of ice or heaviest of snow would keep us from our appointed rounds.

I also switched her to one of the "senior" foods that had recently come on the market. Manufacturers claim these foods are formulated to fit the metabolism and nutritional needs of older dogs, to help combat the tendency to add unwanted weight.

For Annie, these changes did the trick. She soon lost those extra pounds. In fact, her weight held steady between 22 and 23 for the rest of her life, and we never gave up our habit of two or three walks every day. It's funny, but that one morning when I saw her unable to go down a short flight of stairs probably added years of good health to her life. So, in a way, a little back pain turned out to be one of the best things that ever happened to us.

Annie taught me...

A little exercise almost never hurts.
Just let's not go overboard.

And for Annie's Next Trick...

We only lived in the house on Flower Street for a single pleasant year before I would undertake the biggest changes of my life (and Annie's, too): moving to another state, and getting married. Psychologists say that major changes in our lives can cause major stress, even if they're *positive* changes. So our year on Flower Street turned out to be the calm before the storm.

Other than Annie's sore back, it was a nice year. Lynne had grown up with animals, and she and Annie got along well. On those rare occasions when I had to go away and couldn't take Annie along, Lynne took good care of her.

On one of those weekends, Lynne taught Annie a variation on the fetch-game she'd always enjoyed. Lynne's new spin: she sat on the floor, with her crossed legs forming a ring. And when Annie charged after her throw-toy and came racing back with it, Lynne asked Annie to deposit it in the "hoop." Thus was born "Slobber-Basketball."

On another weekend, it was Lynne who had to go out of town. She'd asked me to pick her up at the Long Island Railroad station upon her return. That same afternoon, my parents and my brother Marc and his family had come over for a visit. My sister-in-law Karen had brought over a plate of home-made cookies. When it came time for me to meet Lynne at the train station, we all left the house—except Annie.

We also left the paper plate with Karen's yummy cookies sitting out on the dining room table, which was covered by a tablecloth. After all the years spent with Annie, I should have known better than to leave such temptation within range of her nose. And I should certainly have known better than to underestimate Annie's cleverness and determination when it came to getting food that seemed totally out of reach for a one-foot-tall dog.

When we returned home, we found the paper plate on the dining room carpet. The cookies were gone, with not even a crumb left behind! For a moment, I wondered how Annie had possibly gotten to those cookies. Then I noticed that the table cloth was askew, and I realized Annie had done one of her most masterful magic tricks ever: with her hands, or teeth, or both, she'd reached up...taken hold of the table cloth...and tugged it over until the cookie plate tottered on the table's edge, and finally fell over onto the floor. And Annie had her feast.

The Times They Are a'Changin'

The biggest change in my life during our year on Flower Street was that Susan and I got engaged. Susan T. White: the unsuspecting person doomed to become my wife—but blessed to become Annie's permanent new mommy.

Susan came from Baltimore. She and I had met through our mutual friend (and later my roommate) Lynne a couple of years earlier. They'd come to New York to see a Broadway show and made arrangements to crash on my living-room sofa-bed after their night on the town. Following that visit, starting with the exchange of a couple of letters, Susan and I embarked upon an old-fashioned courtship. First, we became regular penpals, which led to friendship. In the year or so after we'd met, we only saw each other again (and briefly, at that) a couple of times when Annie and I came down to Maryland to be guests at STAR TREK conventions.

Susan had been dating someone. I'd been dating several someones, but no one special. Eventually, we were both unattached at the same time, so I invited her to Long Island for a weekend getting-to-know-you visit. Things rapidly progressed from casual to exclusive. Then, a few months after Annie, Lynne and I moved into the Flower Street house, I proposed to Susan. She said yes. We alternated bi-weekly visits between Baltimore and Long Island for the next several months. But a big decision loomed ahead: which one of us would pack up and relocate to the other's home state?

As often happens with commuter couples, economics played a major role in our decision. Susan had just started her first real, well-paying job as a computer programmer with Bell Atlantic.

And I had only recently quit my job to try full-time freelance writing. Which meant she had a regular paycheck, and I had embarked on a career clouded with uncertainty. Also, I could write from anywhere. So the logical choice made itself clear: At the end of my one-and-only year in that nice rented split-level, I'd uproot my life and move myself and Annie to Maryland.

In the few months preceding my emigration, we had a lot of logistics to keep us busy. In between my writing a novel, and Susan making her way in the working world, we had to plan our moves, consolidate our belongings, figure out what we needed and didn't need, consult on what would soon be our collective finances, and—not least—decide exactly where in Maryland we'd live.

This meant that on my weekend trips south, we spent much of our time checking out the residential possibilities. We eventually settled on the lovely planned-community of Columbia, which hadn't even existed before the first neighborhoods had risen out of rolling farmland back in 1967.

Columbia had several advantages: It was well-located, close to main highways, about 20 minutes south of Baltimore and 45 minutes north of Washington, D.C. Having spent my entire life living in the New York suburbs on Long Island (where the term "Planning & Zoning" unfortunately seemed to mean, "How many shopping malls can we squeeze on one honkin' big island?") I liked the idea of a community where the preservation of green-space was not an alien concept. And Columbia had been purposely designed with a diverse mix of housing throughout the new town. That meant that apartments, attached townhomes and larger single-family houses weren't segregated from each other, as in so many places.

This translated to a wide choice of relatively new and reasonably-priced (by New York standards) apartment complexes, many of which permitted small pets. So the major pieces of our new life together seemed to be falling into place. At the end of the summer of 1989, I packed my car from tail to nose and floor to roof, left Annie her usual space on the floor of the passenger-side front seat, and left everything else I knew behind me.

Annie the Lifeline

Confession: I don't do "*Change*" well. Oh, heck, let's be honest: I *loathe* Change. No matter how much I may logically convince myself that Change may even be a *good* thing, and certainly inevitable, I still end up resisting it every inch of the way. Even smart people can be idiots.

Once things are pretty much OK, why can't they ever just *stay* that way? I mean, why rock the boat? I like maximum certainty and pre-dictability, whenever possible. (At which point, you may be thinking "This guy likes certainty and predictability, so he became a *writer*?! And a *dog-trainer*?!" I've often had that thought myself. And I've decided Bill Gates himself doesn't have enough money to pay for all the therapy that would be needed to sort out my particular personality paradox.)

Of course, I knew all this about myself. Sort of. But for most of the previous ten years prior to moving to Maryland, I'd been able to successfully anchor myself to a pretty steady rock of a life: Same job, same address, etc. Or so I thought.

Sure, there were changes along the way. But they were incremental enough—and manageable enough—that I'd been able to fool myself into thinking I'd mastered the art of peacefully coexisting with Change. I had no inkling whatsoever of just how delusional I was.

Annie had become a big part of my everyday stability. When other things in life quivered and quaked, Annie gave my life structure. She needed to be walked and fed on a regular schedule. I loved playing with and petting her. She was my absolutely-reliable pal and companion. And she was about to become my literal lifeline when Change caught up with me and knocked me flat on my rear end.

Changes? Let me count the ways. In roughly a year, I'd traded a regu-lar if not huge paycheck for the perils of self-employment. I'd been forced to move after living in one place for ten years. I'd done battle with land-lord-attorneys. Then, on top of all that, I was moving yet again—and to a whole new state, away from my varied support system of friends and fam-ily. And I was about to trade bachelorhood for marriage.

On the surface, this is mostly *good* stuff. At the very least, none of it involves disease, disaster or doom.

So why then, almost literally *to the day* I arrived at our new apartment in Maryland, did I fall into a dark, dismal pit of clinical depression?

I don't know.

And since this is a book about dogs, not psychology, I won't spend a lot of time on this topic. But the truth is, I didn't even know I fit the pro-file of someone with clinical depression until Susan brought home a health-care booklet. It had one of those ever-helpful checklists with major symptoms. So there it was, point by point. One day you're fine. The next day—*Bingo!*—you're a dead-ringer for a depressed person.

Of course, it only *seemed* like one day to the next. The reality was, as I kept piling major, stress-inducing changes on top of changes, I finally reached *Overload!* Should I have seen it coming? Who knows. I felt a little like a cartoon character who's just had a giant anvil fall on my head. Now, maybe if I'd been more observant, I'd have seen that anvil hanging up there, by a perilously fraying thread. But I had no reason to suspect there *was* an anvil swinging overhead, so I never even bothered to glance above.

I wasn't suicidal or anything like that. I functioned (sort of). Looking back, I'm astounded at the amount of writing I got done. But it was a real chore to get through each day. Not fun. Not fun at all.

Among the scariest symptoms of depression are inescapable feelings of worthlessness. So, people who know you might still think of you as this reasonably successful, accomplished and together person—while *you* think of yourself as a total failure.

Depression also drains its victims of much of their energy. You become this inert lump. There's the popular image of the loser slumped in front of a TV all day, unwashed, wearing a dingy undershirt and drinking beer after beer. I was *so* pathetic I couldn't even live up to the image: I can't stand to start the day without a good hot shower, I don't wear undershirts and I don't like beer. So *I* had to keep working and *still* be depressed.

As you might imagine, all of this took a toll on our new marriage. Susan thought she was marrying one guy and got his dark twin. I sometimes think she kept me around only because my dog had captured her heart.

· Eventually, Susan and I both sought counseling. Together and separately. Nothing much seemed to help. Not a lot, anyway. Eventually, I did something I'd never, *ever* done in the Psychedelic Sixties and Seventies, when it seemed like everyone around me was trying to get high on one illegal substance or another: I resorted to drugs. Don't worry, these were legal ones. And, *eventually*, after trying a variety of anti-depressant medications, I finally found something that helped me climb back up to a semi-stable plateau.

But I know for an *absolute fact* that I would not have survived that gloomy period of my life without Annie. In the years since, there've been all sorts of news reports about the positive psychological (and even physiological) benefits of having a pet. I'm here to tell you they're all true.

For me, having Annie forced a structure on my life when I didn't feel like doing anything. Without her, gray days would have blurred into one long formless stretch of emptiness. But she needed me to look after her.

In return, she looked after me. You can't explain to a dog what's wrong. She may not understand *why* you're sad, but she knows you *are*.

I didn't want her to think she was the cause of my sadness, so I made an effort (sometimes) to be more cheerful around her—to play with her and pet her and smile at her the way I'd always done before. She'd been the one constant in my life, and now she was in Susan's life, too. When we couldn't understand or felt too lost to talk about what was going on with each other, we focused on Annie.

And she helped us get through the rough times by being what she was: loving and generous; demanding and imperious; a weather-vane sensitive to all our emotions; and a clown who insisted we stop getting so serious over insignificancies and pay attention to what was *really* important— *Annie!*

Annie taught me...

When the going gets tough, pet your dog. No matter what you've lost, if you still have a dog's uncomplicated love, you have a priceless treasure. It may not be a cure-all, but it sure can keep you afloat in a sea of trouble.

Annie's New Mommy

Dogs are instinctively sensitive to the nuances of pack-life, with all its structures of social order. They crave the clarity and certainty that comes with having a single alpha creature in charge. So, dogs are exquisitely designed by nature to live with people. We become their pack. With some training from us, most dogs readily and happily accept secondary status.

Even a smart, assertive dog like Annie can learn to be content with following a human alpha. When she first left her birth family, Annie's pack included me, her Collie "brother" Hawkeye, and Cindi. Even though I was primarily responsible for Annie, and Hawkeye was Cindi's dog, both puppies learned to accept two authority figures. To them, we were essentially interchangeable.

But when Hawk and Cindi moved away, Annie pretty much decided that there would henceforth be only one human to whom she'd defer: me. My next two roommates were more than welcome in her world. She was happy to have someone else to play and socialize with. They could feed her and walk her. But she seemed to regard them as her equals (or even subordinates) in our pack. Not that she wouldn't take commands or instructions from them; but the way she did so convinced me that, as far as she was concerned, she listened because she felt like it, not because she had to.

This made for interesting pack developments when Susan and I moved in together and got married. Susan loved animals in general, and Annie in particular. Like most people, she was charmed by Annie's personality. And Annie was quite taken with Susan. But she often treated Susan like the new puppy in the family.

It also seemed that Annie didn't want to get too close to Susan. Having seen other human pack-mates come and go, Annie may have expected that Susan would do the same. Susan thinks Annie didn't really bond with her until she spent a couple of months unemployed.

During that stretch of time, Susan got to spend all day with Annie, and accompanied us on our daily walks. The quantity and quality of time Susan and Annie enjoyed together seemed to make all the difference. Annie may also have come to the conclusion that Susan wasn't going to be leaving.

After that, one of Annie's favorite activities was "grooming" Susan. Susan would sit on the floor with her, and Annie would start licking Susan's hand. But it wasn't just a cursory greeting, or an exploratory lick to see if Susan tasted of recently-held food. Annie would work on one finger at a time, purposefully cleaning it, licking *between* fingers, then moving on to the next one. She'd lick the palm, right up to the wrist. When she was done, she'd use her nose or paw like a spatula to flip Susan's hand over, and clean the other side.

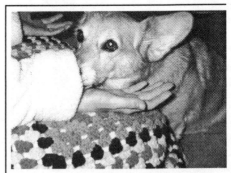

Done licking the hand... let's go right up the sleeve

And Annie did this with total concentration. If I called her name, she'd stop in mid-lick and glance up at me for just a second, then go right back to her precision-licking. Maybe it was her version of a hobby. Whatever else it may have been, it was plainly one of Annie's favorite activities.

"The Attack of the Killer Fleas: The Sequel!"

Fleas are amazing, if repulsive. Outdoors, they can withstand all but the most arctic weather. And the more grass and greenery there is around, the more they thrive. Maryland, I learned soon after my relocation, is something of a Flea Haven since it rarely gets fiercely cold, even in the dead of winter. And when we do have the odd deep freeze, it doesn't persist long enough to smite last year's flea population.

Add to felicitous flea-survival weather the fact that we lived in sylvan Columbia, where good civic planning mandated conservation of surprisingly large stretches of green space. This is one town where they didn't pave Paradise and put up a parking lot. In practical terms, these factors meant "flea season" might last the year 'round. *Uh-oh.*

At first, I tried walking Annie on the little woodsy "island" in the center of the parking area outside our apartment building, hoping it was sufficiently isolated by pavement from the surrounding woods and fields that it might be a flea-free zone. *Ha.* Fat chance.

When that failed, I tried to recreate the solution I'd first invented during that rotten Long Island summer of '84: finding some suitable gravel for Annie to use as her commode. Unfortunately, the nearest such area was a church parking lot a couple of miles down the road. For a few days, I actually bundled Annie into the car every time we had to go out, and drove to that gravel lot. But this was plainly impractical as a long-term solution.

Then Susan and I had an idea. If we couldn't find a convenient patch of gravel, we'd make our own!

We bought a plastic kiddie wading pool, three feet across and about six inches deep. I took the pool out on the balcony of our second-floor apartment, and filled it with alternating layers of soil, gravel and wood chips. I showed it to Annie and she immediately understood this was her very own potty area. Solid waste was easy to clean up and dispose of. And, at least for the cold weather months, the smell of urine was minimal.

Once the weather warmed up, however, we had a problem. Urinating on the ground may kill the grass, but the eliminated liquid seeps into the soil, and rain water helps dilute and disperse it so there's no lingering concentration. Our porch potty-pool was another kettle of fish, so to speak. And smelly fish, too.

The flaw in our otherwise brilliant solution became clear: there was nowhere for all that urine to go, and no way to clean it up. Instead, it saturated the soil and wood chips, and the plastic pool made sure it stayed where it was. By mid-May, the smell could no longer be ignored. The pool would have to be emptied and cleaned.

This was no simple undertaking. The pool contained thirty or forty pounds of material. There was no way to move the full pool down to ground level without risk of spilling the noxious contents. So I had to use a shovel, scoop out the filler, and carry it downstairs one box-full at a time. And if I thought the *surface* odor was objectionable, the ammonia stench from the *bottom* of the pool was *overpowering*. By the time the pool was empty, it was pretty clear there was no way we'd ever get it clean. So we decided to dump it.

But we didn't dump the basic notion of potty pools. It was the only way to protect Annie from flea-torture. So this time, we bought *two* pools. One we lined with layers of newspapers, to serve as Annie's urinal. Paper was easy to remove after each potty visit, so we completely avoided the smell problem. The other pool we filled with shallow layers of gravel and wood chips, and that's where she pooped.

Believe it or not, this revised system actually worked. Annie could go to the bathroom without exposure to fleas. There was just one drawback. Our balcony was not perfectly level. So when Annie hopped into the pee-pool and did her thing, urine inevitably trickled downhill. It was almost impossible for her to relieve herself without getting some urine on her feet or fur. So I'd have to carry her immediately into the real bathroom and clean her up. To Annie's great credit, she put up with this on-going indignity without complaint.

So that's how we managed to keep the fleas at bay. But I don't know if we could have gone to such lengths indefinitely.

As it turned out, we didn't have to.

The Strangest Reason
Anybody Ever Bought a House

As our rent climbed higher, it dawned on us that we could probably afford a small home of our own for the same monthly payment. So Susan and I started house-hunting.

Like most first-time buyers, we juggled a bunch of variables. Objective factors included price, location, floorplan, and practicality. If you've ever bought a house, you also know there's an equally important subjective consideration, one that can actually be decisive: does the house *feel* right?

We looked at lots of houses, all over central Maryland. We liked the area where we already were, in or around Columbia. And we were forced to admit we could only afford an attached townhome, rather than a free-standing single-family dwelling. The more models we strolled through, the more we refined what we liked and didn't like.

And we kept coming back to one particular model. The house was a three-floor design, with a one-car garage at ground level. It had a little postage-stamp lawn out front. A full L-shaped flight of concrete-and-brick steps led from the driveway up to the main-level front door. And nestled between the blacktopped driveway and the steps was a rectangular patch of dirt, where an ornamental shrub would be planted as part of the standard landscaping package.

Hold on! I took one look at that four-foot-by-six plot, and realized it was completely surrounded by flea-barrier materials. Blacktop on one side, concrete and brick on the other three. We could tell the builder to put that shrub someplace else. We could cover the dirt with patio bricks to keep urine from seeping into the ground. We could pour decorative gravel over the patio bricks. Even better, the outdoor water faucet was close at hand, so we'd be able to hose the area down on a regular basis. We would have the potty area of our dreams.

And the *house* was pretty good, too.

So we bought it (with financial assistance from my parents).

When we moved in, Annie went right to her potty place like she'd designed it herself. And the fleas were out of luck.

At our new house, Annie chews her bone inside her new "fortress"

Annie taught me...

When you're responsible for a little furry life, you should be willing to do anything short of murder and mayhem to keep that life free from unnecessary suffering.

Flea-Fighting

When it comes to the age-old conflict against fleas, today's dogs benefit from better living through chemistry. Pharmaceutical companies have come up with a range of products that are less toxic to us and our dogs—and *more* toxic to fleas and ticks.

🐾 Forget the old flea-collars, powders, sprays and shampoos. If you're not already using the most recent anti-flea pills and "spot-on" ointments, do yourself and your pooch a favor and talk to your vet. They really work!

🐾 We may not have won the war, but at least we've got some effective weapons to give us a chance to take the lead in the battle.

Annie's Bench

One of the nice features of our new house was the box-bay window in our living room. It gave us some extra floor space, and a front view of the neighborhood. Dogs naturally like to look out windows.

For a Corgi, however, that can sometimes be tough. When you're roughly one foot tall, windows have to be pretty low for you to see out, unassisted. Annie had never lived with such a window. Fortunately, the trend in new homes is toward ever-larger windows. Unfortunately for Annie, the bottom sill in our box-bay was still too high, at fourteen inches, for her to see out without jumping up.

As soon as we moved in, she checked out the window. And she discovered she could see out, if she put her hands up on the sill moulding. Rather than have her destroy the trim with her nails, we found her a little wooden bench for five bucks at an antiques flea market. I upholstered it with some quilted cloth so she wouldn't slip, and placed it in front of the window.

Then I called her over and invited her to take a step up. She discovered that the extra six inches of lift let her see out perfectly. She could balance on it as long as she wanted, whenever she felt the need to keep an eye on what was happening outside. Every evening, when she knew it was time for Susan to come home, Annie would go to her bench and keep watch. And now her successors Mickey and Callie do the very same thing.

Nesting

Annie was nine when we moved into our little townhome on its pleasant court. As she aged gracefully, she spent more and more of her day napping. Since she'd never been allowed on our furniture, we decided it was time she had her own. For the bedroom upstairs, we got her an *L.L. Bean* dog bed. For the living room, where we usually spent our evenings watching television or listening to music, we gave her a nice, soft pillow and an old towel.

Dogs like to nest. It's an instinctive activity, and they'll do it on any surface, hard or soft. They'll knead it with their hands, then tightly circle the chosen spot a few times, until it feels just right.

Annie elevated nesting to a fine art. While Susan and I would settle into our matching recliners with a minimum of fussing, Annie was just getting started. A typical session went something like this:

She'd use paws and teeth to arrange the towel on top of the pillow. She'd punch and scrunch the pillow, fluffing it to just the right shape. She'd lie down. And decide it *wasn't* right after all. She'd climb out and use her hands to push and pull the whole pillow across the living room carpet. Then she'd set about rearranging the bedding. She'd test it yet again. Stay for a few seconds. Then climb out and do some *more* fine-tuning.

Sometimes this went on for fifteen minutes, with the bed migrating halfway across the room until both position and shape satisfied our demanding little dog. Only *then* would Annie settle down for a contented nap.

Time for a nap…

Nesting is hard work.
Now, if you'll excuse me…

…I'll bury my nose and see you later.

Annie taught me...

If you're in a lousy mood, just watch your dog sleep. Stretched out or curled up, sleeping dogs look so angelic, they're almost guaranteed to make you smile.

Sunbeams

I remember an old *Peanuts* comic strip, with Snoopy declaring that dogs were born to eat, and sleep in the sun. Annie agreed with that philosophy wholeheartedly. If there are any dogs out there who disagree, I have yet to meet one.

Whenever there was a patch of sunshine on the floor, Annie would find it and nap in the golden glow. And she'd follow it, too, as it crept across the room as the day wore on toward evening.

One afternoon, watching our dog bask, Susan christened Annie as her "Sunbeam." And she was, in the sense that sunbeams brighten the darkest days.

Dogs know instinctively what we too often forget, what with our frenetic lives and overbooked schedules: that there are few greater satisfactions than a full belly and a nap in the sun. I think the dogs are onto something, don't you?

Telling Time

For years, experts have claimed that dogs have no meaningful sense of time, that they react the same way whether you're gone for five minutes or five days. My observations have convinced me quite the opposite. Even though I have no quantifiable science to back this up, I have no doubts that many dogs do indeed have a keen sense of time and very accurate internal clocks. I know Annie did.

First of all, if we feed them at the same times each day (or do anything else on a regular schedule) dogs know this and expect us to stick to that schedule. Back in the days when I commuted to work in New York City, Annie had to wait until I made the long trek home before she'd be fed.

Once I started working at home, I advanced her dinnertime to roughly four in the afternoon.

And, without fail, no matter where she might be or what she might be doing, her stomach-clock went off an hour before meal-time. From three o'clock on, she'd shadow me, hoping her presence would convince me it was time to feed her NOW! She didn't pester me, cry, or beg. She'd just *stare* at me, *willing* me to go dish out and serve her chow.... NOW!

It's easy to see why she continued this behavior. As far as she could tell, it eventually delivered the desired results. She didn't really know I would have fed her at the same time, even without her reminding me. Her reasoning was clear: *I stare at Daddy, and he feeds me.* Corgi cause-and-effect.

I see the same thing with Annie's successors, Mickey and Callie. In addition to exercising mealtime mind-control over me, Mickey and Callie have two other evening activities to anticipate.

The first comes at about 6:30 each night, when we put a dozen pieces of dry dog kibble into a special soft-plastic toy called a *Tricky Treats* ball. When it's pushed around the floor, the ball dispenses the food nuggets one or two at a time, at unpredictable intervals.

Callie does all the ball-rolling, and gets most of the food rewards. Mickey tags along. But, starting roughly an hour before ball-time, the dogs go to where the ball is kept, and alternately stare at us and the ball, trying to get us to give them what they want.

Actually, we had to temporarily suspend *Tricky Treats* play. Callie rolled the ball so vigorously that she rubbed the hair and pigment off a spot just above the black part of her nose, and developed a callous! So we invented a *new* special activity for 6:30: peanut butter carrot bones!

These are small hollow white bones, about 3 or 4 inches long. (You can get these at almost any pet supply store.) We fill one end of the bone's center cavity with smooth peanut butter. Then we take those neat little pre-peeled, ready-to-eat carrots sold in grocery produce sections, and we wedge one halfway in each bone, solidly held in place by the gooey peanut butter. The doggies literally run into their crates to await this treat.

First, they have to pull the carrot out of the peanut butter. Carrots are okay for dogs to crunch and eat. Then they spend the next 15 minutes or so licking all the peanut butter out of the bone. And they only get this treat once a day, and always in their crates—which helps to remind them that the crate is a nice place to be...which in turn makes it easy for us to get them into their crates whenever we need to do so.

The next highlight of their evening comes at eight o'clock, when we go into the kitchen and give them a second special treat—a chunk of carrot-bone (no, carrots don't have bones, but these are chew toys made mostly of carrot). By that time of night, we're usually in the living room, watching TV. And the dogs, resting on the living room floor, keep sharp eyes on us. If it's close to eight, and I make any move that looks like I might get out of my recliner, those dogs instantaneously jump up and dart toward the kitchen like a synchronized school of fish, anticipating their next gastronomic delight.

So maybe dogs can't tell you it's 11:58 and 12 seconds, Eastern Standard Time. But don't tell me dogs have no sense of time.

Once, when I had to be away from home for four days, Susan found that Annie seemed to grasp an even more complex chronological concept: *Tomorrow*. As the days passed, Annie knew I wasn't there. The night before I came home, Susan told her, "Daddy will be home *tomorrow*."

Sure enough, the next morning, when she heard Susan waking up, literal-minded Annie raced directly to my side of the bed, fully expecting that I'd be there. Annie hadn't done this on any of the previous three mornings, but only after Mommy had told her I'd be home "*tomorrow*." Pretty amazing.

Food VI:
Table Manners

A few years after I'd moved to Maryland, old pal Cindi came to the Washington, D.C. area on a business trip. One evening, Susan, Annie and I took a drive out toward Dulles Airport to visit Cindi at her hotel.

Susan and I had already eaten dinner at home, and Cindi had ordered a room-service soup-and-sandwich platter. By the time we arrived, she'd eaten the soup and half the sandwich. She'd resealed the other half of the sandwich in its clingy plastic wrap, and stuck the usual deli-style tasseled toothpick through the bread.

The empty soup bowl and half-sandwich sat on their tray upon the hotel-room desk.

After we played with Annie and chatted for a while, we decided to head out to a local mall restaurant for a snack. We left Annie in the room.

An hour or so later, we returned to find Annie resting on the floor, waiting for us as quietly and calmly as usual.

Then Cindi happened to glance at her room-service tray. She did a double-take. Of course, the remaining half-sandwich was gone. That Annie had clambered up on the desk chair (no easy task for a Corgi) and done away with the leftovers was not a great surprise.

Ahh, but the *way* she'd done it! The plastic wrapping had been meticulously opened, not shredded, and the toothpick set aside with care—all without so much as a stray toothmark or wayward crumb.

If a detective had examined that tray, he would have concluded that some unknown *person* had entered the room and polished off Cindi's sandwich. But we knew the truth: the culprit was a little person in a doggie suit.

Annie taught me...

We all deserve to be forgiven
for surrendering to temptation
now and then.

Food VII:
Jaws May Be Closer Than They Appear

Not that Annie's table manners were *always* so impeccable. On our car trips, I'd usually drive, Susan sat up front, and Annie had the back seat to herself. We'd set her up with her bed-pillow and nesting towel. And she'd either watch the scenery go by, or nap. Some dogs hate car rides. Annie— happily for us—was a naturally relaxed traveller.

Except when food entered the picture. Big surprise there. Whether we pulled off at a rest stop for lunch, or simply unzipped the food bag for a snack en route, Annie always requested her share. Firmly.

Since it wasn't really fair to tease her with our food, we always had treats and biscuits for her, too. Per usual practice, we'd give her one of her snacks at the same time as we had ours.

On one trip, Susan reached for the food bag, and took out a big slice of fresh, fragrant raisin bread. This was too much temptation for Annie. When Susan turned around to peek at her between the bucket seats, Annie was ready to pounce. With one lightning-quick motion, she grabbed the other end of the bread and snatched it right out of Susan's mouth.

By the time we reacted (with laughter, I must admit), Annie had already gobbled up most of the bread. She wore a slightly guilty "oops" expression, as if she knew it wasn't quite proper to yank food out of Mommy's mouth. But she also knew we understood that, when it came to food dangling so close at tooth, sometimes her mouth just had a mind of its own.

Annie taught me…

We all deserve to be forgiven
for surrendering to temptation
now and then…
and again.

Grand-Dog

Annie genuinely enjoyed our trips back to New York to visit my parents. Considering her status as beloved grand-dog, this comes as no surprise.

As I mentioned earlier, Annie was the first dog anyone in my immediate family had ever known well. None of us had any inkling that a dog could be so well-behaved and so completely captivating. As I came to love Annie, so did my parents. She was always considered a true member of the family.

Back in the early days, there loomed one major obstacle to this: my father's allergy. He and Annie couldn't really be in the same indoor confines without his having a severe reaction that would persist well after separation. Even if I came to my parents' house without my dog, the dander I carried on my clothing would be enough to start Dad sneezing.

So, nice man that he is, my father went to his allergist and asked for a solution. The doctor suggested using the hair of the dog—and I'm not referring to the old remedy for a hangover. He quite literally meant the hair of *this* particular dog. Annie donated a cup of fur, which the allergist used to concoct a specific injection serum designed to desensitize my father to the allergens in Annie's dander.

It worked. Thanks to my father's thoughtfulness, not only could Annie go to my parents' house, but they could even come to my house with all the dander and dog hair more or less omnipresent in Annie's home environment.

Once the allergy hitch had been hurdled, Annie was included in all family gatherings. My mother would proudly show Annie off to relatives and friends, praising her good nature and intelligence. She seemed to take special delight in having us run through Annie's repertoire of tricks. And Annie always gave a joyful and flawless performance.

Annie's favorite hangout at my mother's house was the kitchen. We'd pull into the driveway and get out of the car. The second her feet hit the ground, Annie would dash up the path, up the steps, into the house (barely pausing for the door to be opened) and straight to the kitchen with all the unswerving resolve of a Derby champion flying toward the finish line.

Now, you may recall my mentioning that my mother has always maintained a spotless home. But dogs are the very embodiment of hope, and Annie never failed to sniff every corner of that kitchen in search of Corgicules of whatever my mother had been cooking in preparation for our arrival.

On Thanksgiving, I would half-expect Annie to climb right into the oven with that juicy turkey. And it's a wonder, with Annie dogging her every step, that Mom never tripped over her.

Annie had learned through years of practice that her persistence in my mother's kitchen would eventually be rewarded. On our occasional weekend excursions from Maryland, it sometimes seemed as if I spent most of my time scolding my parents with endless repetitive variations on a single phrase: "No, you *can't* give her _____" (fill in the blank with all sorts of food).

I confess that I did give Annie an occasional tidbit of human food. When I cooked steaks, I'd cut up the fatty scraps and add a couple of morsels to each of her regular meals over the next few days. When I added raisins to my breakfast cereal, Annie would get one raisin.

But I do believe my mother would only have been satisfied with permission to serve Annie a full meal of whatever we were having. Plus seconds.

Over and over, I'd patiently (okay, not always patiently) explain that 1) giving table scraps directly from human plates turns dogs into obnoxious little beggars; and 2) human food isn't really good for dogs. Some of it is downright toxic (chocolate, for instance), while some merely causes vomiting and diarrhea. Fun.

To their credit, my parents generally abided by my ruling on this subject. Dad would happily flip Annie a raisin or a Cheerio at breakfast, wishing he could give her more. Mom did the same, and otherwise stuck to letting Annie lick her fingers after she ate something tasty.

Usually.

Every now and then, when I wasn't present to stop it, Mom would "accidentally" drop a morsel of chicken or turkey on the kitchen floor. Annie would capture and eat it before it could escape. And I'd roll my eyes in the next room. Grandparents. What're you gonna do with 'em?

What I didn't know was that Annie and my mother had evolved a signal for these illicit treats. This didn't dawn on me until after we'd returned to Maryland from one of our visits north. Annie was in our living room, minding her own business. I was in the kitchen, doing something that had no connection with food. When I dropped something non-edible, I reflexively said, "*Ooops.*"

And Annie galloped in, skittering around the corner, wearing her "Where's the beef?" face. It took a second for me to figure out the chain of events: "*Ooops*" was what my mother always said, in a tone of exaggerated innocence, every time she made an unauthorized food-drop for Annie.

Annie knew the word. Knew what it meant. And I started laughing the instant I realized how my mother had trained Annie without even knowing it. Or was it Annie who'd trained Grandma?

Annie taught me...

Old dogs can learn new tricks. So can people. The way my parents learned to love Annie and the affection they always showered on her almost make up for Mom throwing away my baseball cards. (Just kidding, Mom!)

Annie Goes to College

Annie was such a good traveling companion that I hated to leave her behind. Those few times we were separated by days and miles, I don't know which of us missed the other more. One of our longest trips was a drive from Maryland to Massachusetts, for a *STAR TREK* convention in Springfield. On the way back south, I made a stop at my alma mater, the University of Connecticut, to visit Thomas J. Roberts, PhD.

Tom was the one college teacher with whom I'd remained in touch. A genial English professor with a dry wit, he seemed genuinely interested in what happened to his students after they'd graduated and moved on into the big, bad Real World. More than merely a former teacher, I considered Tom a friend, and I was pleased and honored when he invited me back on several occasions to talk to his current classes in science fiction and graphic novels/comic books.

Once we arrived, since I didn't want to leave Annie in the car, she went with me to the classroom building. As we walked across campus, I was amazed at how many attractive young women stopped to pet her and, incidentally, talk to me.

Annie taught me...

If I'd only known during college the effect
that cute dogs have on cute young women,
I'd have gotten a puppy way back then.
Ahhh, hindsight.

Coldcut Tongue

When Annie got tired, the tip of her pink tongue would creep out of her mouth. A little like a snake's tongue. But not forked. And much cuter. And it didn't move. It didn't do anything. It just stuck out.

By the time she'd fall asleep, a good half inch would be visible. The longer she slept, the more dry her tongue-tip would become. Eventually, it would sort of pucker. And it would resemble a little dessicated piece of pink ham.

Felt like it, too.

Yes, you could touch it gently and not even wake Annie up.

I never did figure out why Annie's tongue stuck out like that when she napped. And I don't know if this is something all dogs do, or certain breeds, or whether it's unique to certain individual dogs. But I do have a theory. Considering Annie's love affair with food, I think her tongue acted as an early-warning system. Snake tongues flick out and "smell" the air. I think Annie's tongue did the same thing (except for the flicking) while she was asleep.

If anything edible entered her immediate environment, well, that was like a call to duty for a dog like Annie. And her early-warning tongue-tip would sense the presence of food and wake the rest of her up.

I can't prove any of this. But knowing Annie, it's a plausible explanation. And it looked so darned cute.

Fritos Puppy

Have you ever smelled *Fritos* Corn Chips? It's hard to describe. It's sweet and salty, just a little bit greasy, and pretty much irresistible all at the same time. It's also what Annie smelled like after she'd been sleeping for a while.

Most dogs have some kind of natural aroma. In some cases, it's just a hint of a scent. In others, it could be enough to stop a charging elephant at twenty paces.

Many dog-owners react to *any* smell by assuming their dogs need baths. Dogs are not children; they're supposed to smell (somewhat, anyway). In a misguided attempt to deodorize our pets, lots of us are guilty of overbathing them. This can lead to dry skin, excessive itching and dandruff—and for all that effort, the smell may remain.

Unless you've got a dog who likes to roll in the mud, regular grooming is better than frequent baths.

Other than a few flea baths, Annie never had a bath in her life. Corgis generally aren't an objectionably-smelly breed. In fact, Annie's only doggy scent was this Fritos smell. And that was actually quite pleasant.

Apparently, some other Corgi owners discover the same thing about their dogs. But it doesn't seem to be universal. I guess we were just lucky.

"Klingons"

I mentioned earlier that I've written many *STAR TREK* stories over the years (for television, novels and comic books). Not everyone is a *STAR TREK* fan. But almost everyone seems to know of *STAR TREK*. Since the original TV series began in 1966, STAR TREK has become a permanent pop-culture icon.

STAR TREK's characters (and the actors who've played them) have become beloved figures of modern myth. References to *STAR TREK* abound in seemingly unrelated areas of our world, and its terminology has infiltrated our common language: even people who've never seen a single episode or movie, folks who wouldn't know a Klingon from a Vulcan, *do* know such phrases as "Beam me up, Scotty" (which Captain Kirk apparently never actually said, much as Humphrey Bogart's Rick never actually said "Play it again, Sam" in *Casablanca*).

And, speaking of Klingons...

Every now and then, as Annie scoured our floors for anything edible, she'd ingest one of Susan's longish hairs. (Dogs shed, and so do we.) Human hair is astonishingly tough, and essentially undigestible. So any long hairs Annie might eat would course their way through her pipes, unscathed along the way by powerful digestive juices. It would—how can I put this delicately?—take its place within the line of waste materials waiting to be ejected as what we shall refer to as, umm, *dog poop*.

Then a funny thing would happen. As chunks of poop made their exit from Annie's stern, an occasional piece would come out attached to a long strand of hair—the *other* end of which would still be attached to what remained inside. The result: a dangling poop chunk. Annie hated this. She'd buck and twist and two-step, trying to dislodge that which stubbornly hung on, quite literally, by a thread.

At this point, she'd usually require some assistance, provided by a friendly hand gloved within a plastic bag. Such phenomena beg—no, they *demand*—to be named. So what should we end up calling a piece of poop clinging onto a dog's rear end? Why, none other than a "*Klingon.*" Get it? "*Cling-on*"?

We thought we were being original. We've since learned to our great delight that other dog-owners have come to the same conclusion. And *STAR TREK* makes its presence felt in yet another peculiar yet rather logical way.

*Look at that grin! At 11 weeks,
ready to rule the world.*

*6-month-old Annie strikes
a winsome sunset pose*

My 4-year-old niece Kimberly gets a surprise kiss from Annie

Classic Corgi:
The Bold and the Beautiful…Annie

Annie with her best little pal Michele
Wright (and Michele's mom Mary Ann)

Annie waits on the "Mommy-Watch" bench

*Annie rests on her sick-bed, guarded by the hot-pink dragon
Michele brought to cheer up her furry friend*

*Susan hugs two tiny Corgis (the pup on
the right would soon be our Callie)*

Baby Cal-Cal

Furry Christmas angels Callie and Mickey

*No one could fill Annie's shoes. All Mickey and Callie
have to do is be their own unique little selves.
We're lucky to have them.*

Part Three
TWILIGHT

Lucky Thirteen

When Annie reached her thirteenth birthday, I relaxed (a little), knowing that my puppy had reached a ripe old age.

Some dogs, especially smaller breeds, live on into their late teens. But many, regardless of breed, die well before that age, susceptible as are people to a frightening array of diseases and conditions.

Not only had Annie reached thirteen, but she was still in great shape. Sure, she'd gone a little gray around the muzzle. And she spent a greater portion of her day napping. Her eyesight wasn't what it used to be; she could no longer pick out a single grain of white rice on a white floor from twenty paces.

And her hearing acuity had slipped. Where once the distant sound of the UPS truck turning onto our block would prompt an instant-alert bark, now the truck could drive right past our house without a peep from her. My office is upstairs in our house. And with the computer humming, there were times when our doorbell rang and I wouldn't hear it. But I had always been able to count on Annie to bark at the sound of anyone at our front door. And since she rarely barked without good reason, her call would let me know something was happening. After thirteen, she'd often sleep through the chime of the doorbell.

These changes were all unmistakable signs of old age. And I couldn't see them without feeling melancholy, knowing they meant that time was running out. And there wasn't much I could do about that.

But throughout my life, I'd seen old dogs that really looked and acted *old*. They'd become gray and overweight, and moved slowly as age and arthritis took a toll on their entire bodies. Decline seemed inevitable, and it could be heart-breaking to watch.

But Annie after age thirteen was a different story. Overall, she'd weathered the years well. Lifestyle changes helped: more exercise, reduced food portions, and a switch to "lite" dog food geared for elderly pups. Thanks to our care and her own strong constitution, she still had spring in her step and played with all the joyous energy of a puppy.

Around that time, I subscribed to a holistic veterinary newsletter. While I'm skeptical about alternative medicine, I also try to be open-minded. And some of the information in this newsletter made sense. An article about dog food talked about how many preservatives and chemicals were in most commercial dog foods, some of them known carcinogens. So we switched Annie to a top-quality "natural" food.

Soon after, she suddenly started having trouble getting up the stairs of our three-story townhome. There didn't seem to be any definite physical reason. She didn't have arthritis. She wasn't in any specific pain. We worried that the inevitable decline she'd avoided for so long had finally caught up with her.

Then we decided to try something else suggested in that holistic newsletter. We started putting shredded raw carrots and celery into her food. Our vet didn't know if it would help, but we all figured it couldn't hurt.

Within a month, the change was nothing short of miraculous. Annie resumed bounding up and down the steps like her old self. Or should I say *young* self. I don't know why the raw veggies worked. I can't even say, scientifically, that the dietary supplement was *the* factor that made the difference. And I won't tell you to do what we did. But the veggies were the one change we made. And the results were amazing.

I said earlier that I relaxed when she hit thirteen. In my mind, thirteen was an important milestone. It signified that she'd lived a good, long and happy life. Anything after that was bonus time. We wanted her to be with us forever, of course, but we knew that was impossible. We were determined to do whatever we could to keep her as healthy as we could. But sooner or later, time would run out.

Annie's Last Battle

We knew that Annie would eventually face a health crisis that couldn't be overcome.

It happened two months shy of her fifteenth birthday. Susan and I were getting ready to drive up to New York to visit my parents. A few days before we were to leave, Susan was petting Annie—and found a small hard lump on her neck, below her ear. We tried to tell ourselves that Annie had already had a variety of lumps and cysts that had turned out to be nothing serious. Still, with a dog Annie's age, the first thing you think of when you find a lump is... *cancer*. So we called our vet, Dr. David Tayman, and he suggested we bring her in for an examination.

After he checked her, Dr. Tayman tried to be optimistic. It was impossible to tell much about the lump just from feeling it. It might be a simple swelling due to infection. It might be another one of her benign cysts. To be safe, they did a needle biopsy. The lab results wouldn't be back for a couple of days. So we packed up and went to New York on Friday, as planned. We decided we wouldn't mention anything to my parents, who loved Annie as much as we did. We didn't want them to worry over what we hoped would be nothing.

When we got to my parents' house, I made a private call to the vet's office. Dr. Tayman told me the lab results were "inconclusive." They didn't show anything definitive, one way or the other (meaning, no identifiable cancer cells were found). But there were some abnormal cells. He still hoped it would prove to be an infection and prescribed a round of antibiotics.

Susan and I chose to look on the bright side, to believe our magic little Annie had dodged another bullet. And we told my parents what was going on, and enjoyed the weekend visit with them.

All through the following week, we kept feeling the lump. We wanted to find it getting smaller. It didn't cooperate. When we brought Annie back to the vet at the end of the week, he thought the lump had grown larger instead. Clearly, it was not an infection. And our spirits sank.

A second needle biopsy was done. This time, the results were definite: cancer. Annie would have to undergo exploratory surgery. Dr. Tayman hoped the tumor would be something that could be removed. But he wouldn't know for certain until he could see what was there.

It became harder and harder to be hopeful. This time, Annie's number had come up, as it eventually does for all of us.

We waited for the post-surgical news. And it wasn't good. The tumor turned out to be in one of Annie's salivary glands, and it involved too many blood vessels to be operable. Dr. Tayman had removed as much of it as he could, then stitched her up again.

And there was more bad news. An X-ray revealed a shadow in her chest. This indicated that the cancer, undetectable a scant few weeks before, had apparently already spread. Our options were limited.

Pets now routinely receive treatments similar to humans. This is good if you have a sick animal. But such cutting-edge treatments are not as readily available for pets as for people. We learned that veterinary hospitals equipped to provide radiation therapy are still uncommon. We would have had to take Annie out of state and leave her there for a while. We had to rule that out. Not only did we not want to be separated from her, but the treatment would be extremely expensive.

That left two choices. We could do nothing. Which wasn't a choice at all. Dr. Tayman told us Annie's cancer was among the most aggressive he'd ever seen in a dog. Left untreated, it would spread, and quickly. She'd have at most only a few weeks left, and she'd probably be in pain.

So the only real choice was chemotherapy. We could take Annie to a veterinary cancer specialist an hour or so from where we lived. Or Dr. Tayman could consult with the specialist and administer the chemo treatments in his office. This would also be expensive. Susan and I immediately agreed: whatever the cost, we had to try this, to give Annie a fighting chance.

Even at her age, and with cancer already spreading, Annie bounced back from her surgery in a matter of days. She looked awful, with a huge swatch of her lush fur coat shaved away from her neck and face, baring the stitched scar and the small plastic shunt-tube that allowed the wound to drain. But she was up and about, with an eager appetite. She was even strong enough to take short strolls in front of our house.

The chemo treatment was another story. Dr. Tayman had explained to us that reactions to chemotherapy could vary widely and unpredictably from one individual to another. After all, chemotherapy essentially administers a hefty dose of a toxic substance, in hopes of knocking out the disease without knocking out the patient.

The first few days after the treatment, Annie had no appetite at all. Weak and sickly, for the first time she looked like a dog running out of time. Intravenous fluids kept her from becoming dehydrated. We waited for her appetite to revive. It didn't.

I cooked up her all-time favorite treat—fresh, juicy steak. For the first time in her life, she got the *meat* instead of the *scraps*. And she actually ate some!

That development gave us some hope. But it was short-lived. Although she ate her special steak with surprising gusto, she couldn't keep it down. And although the chemotherapy agent reduced the tumor itself to almost nothing in the space of a week, it had also taken an irreparable toll on her ageing organs, especially her liver.

Her indestructible little system had met its match.

And we had no choice but to prepare for the inevitable.

The Music Box

I've written and read science fiction and fantasy stories for years. I hope there really are extraterrestrial life forms somewhere out in the vast Universe. I freely admit to enjoying TV shows like *THE X FILES*. But I don't think we've been visited by E.T. yet, and I'm reasonably certain the only people helped by psychic hotlines are the ones who collect the outrageous fees inflicted on gullible callers.

Having said all that, I have absolutely no explanation for the *TWILIGHT ZONE*-ish thing that happened during the night of May 1, 1996, a little more than a week before Annie died. Let me tell you the story.

Some years earlier, I'd been given the gift of a snow-globe music box. It came from the nice folks who organized Shore Leave, the annual Baltimore *STAR TREK* convention at which I'd been a guest speaker for many years, and to which Annie had come with me for most of her life. Atop the glass globe was a sleeping dog with a peaceful expression on her face. Inside the globe was the same dog, wide awake and smiling, with a ball and chew-bone at her feet. Wind it up, and the music box plays "*My Favorite Things.*"

It was a very thoughtful gift, and we placed that music box, along with our other doggie knickknacks on the plant shelf alongside the staircase leading from our living room up to our top floor.

The days while Annie was sick were difficult. But the nights were worse. Annie seemed to sleep well enough. We didn't. Though neither Susan nor I said anything to each other, we feared that Annie would pass away during the night, and we wouldn't discover it until we got up in the morning.

Yes, we feared that. But part of each of us also wished that Annie be granted such a peaceful death, one which relieved us of the awful responsibility of deciding when to end her suffering by having her euthanized.

Whichever of us woke up during the night would pad over and check to make sure Annie was still breathing.

One night, at one of the rare times when we both slept soundly, we were suddenly awakened by the music box playing from the hallway. At most, it played an eerie half-dozen notes. Slowly. Distinctly separated. As if the music box were winding down.

The magical mystical musical snow globe

Susan got up and rushed over to Annie's corner of our bedroom. She whispered to me that Annie's fur felt cold. I hurried over. Susan was right. For a moment, we both thought the end had come. I shook Annie gently. There was no reaction.

I shook her again.

Finally, she moved. She was still alive. We wrapped her gently in her blanket to keep her warm. And we tried to go back to sleep.

There's no reason on earth why that music box should have made a sound. No one had wound it for years prior to that night. And yet it played. To this day, Susan believes Annie might have slipped away that night had the music box not called out to us. But we weren't ready to let her go.

In a way, I envy people who go through life convinced that a heavenly afterlife awaits them. It must make this earthly life easier. But there's one thing of which I am sure: if there is a heaven, dogs certainly go there.

People who've had the pleasure of the company of a dog know that dogs are good and pure of heart, wanting nothing more than to share their lives with human companions who take good care of them and are kind to them. They have so much to teach us about patience and forgiveness, if only we're willing to learn. They make us better people.

There's no devotion like a dog's devotion. And if any creatures *deserve* to go to a heaven, dogs do.

So the non-rational part of me wondered if the notes from that mystical music box came from Hawkeye, the Collie who had been Annie's puppyhood pal. Hawkeye had died much too young, at age eight. He was the only dog-friend Annie had ever truly loved. Maybe he was calling to her from "the other side." I really don't know.

But I do know this: that music box had *never* played all by itself before. And it's never done so *since*.

Dogs Know When to Go

During Annie's last week, I knew the time was fast approaching when we'd have to make the decision to end her suffering. Though my voice came out in a shaky whisper, I finally asked Dr. Tayman the question I'd dreaded the most: *How will we know when it's time?*

I guess that's the toughest question for any vet, yet they must hear it dozens of times a year. Dr. Tayman didn't give me a scientific answer, but a spiritual one. He quietly said, "She'll let you know."

And she did. She couldn't eat. She was too weak to even stand, much less walk. Several times each day, I had to wrap her in her towel and carry her outside to go to the bathroom. Susan took off from work so we could both spend as much time as possible sitting with her, talking to her and touching her. We could see her growing thin and frail. And we knew she was not going to get better.

We have this friend named Alan Chafin. I've known him for years. He's a good person with a big heart. And, having been fortunate enough to grow up with a family dog named Boots who sounds like he was quite a character, Alan loves dogs.

Also, owing to a peripatetic childhood as a Navy brat (and some globe-trotting time in the service himself) Alan has this disconcerting penchant for up and moving to farflung parts of the country for (what I consider) no particularly good reason.

At one point, he'd decided to return to Maryland from a self-inflicted tour of hard time in rural Blacksburg, Virginia. The plan was to come back and get a job—almost any job—and an apartment. Ahh, but there was a catch: nobody would rent him an apartment until he had a visible means of support. He figured he could get a job fairly quickly, but needed a place to stay in the meantime. So we invited him to bunk in our basement, which he did for a few weeks. And he not only had a place to stay. He also got an unexpected bonus: each morning, Annie would run downstairs to wake him up with puppy kisses. Each night, she'd come down to make sure he was there.

And even after he moved out, she'd go downstairs to see if maybe he'd come back. Annie had known Alan before, but they developed a special bond during his time as our houseguest. She was a good judge of character—especially if the character in question understood the importance of stopping to pet Annie long and often. Alan did.

When Annie got sick, he followed her medical progress with the concern of a family member. And he asked me to let him know when I thought we were nearing the end. He wanted to be able to say a proper goodbye. I promised I would tell him.

One day during that last week, when I had to leave Annie at the vet's office for a few hours of tests and intravenous nutrients, Alan came over to join me for lunch, and to go with me to the vet. This would be his final chance to see Annie, and to lend me some moral support.

But when Alan saw Annie looking so sad and sick, his emotions got the better of him. I saw tears welling up in his eyes as he petted his friend one last time. "Some moral support you turn out to be, tough guy," I grumbled.

So Susan and I faced the truth: Annie's life was drawing to a close. We decided early in the week, barring a miracle, that Saturday would be the day. But Annie silently asked us to let her go a day earlier. Though she seemed to be in no obvious pain, we could see she had no fight left in her. Instead, we saw peace. So we changed our appointment to Friday.

Driving her to the vet for that final trip was the hardest thing I've ever had to do. Somehow, I kept a stoic lid on my emotions. I didn't want Annie to think she wasn't making us happy, even though our hearts were breaking.

She died in our arms. And we carried her home one last time.

Near the end, I carry Annie outside to go to the bathroom. We were thankful she never seemed to be in pain.

Annie taught me...

Part of loving (the last part, I suppose) is letting go of the one you love. Losing the loved one doesn't mean losing the love. But it sure does hurt. I hate this lesson.

Annie's Final Gift

We loved Annie so much that we knew we could never replace her. But we also knew we couldn't live without the joy she gave us every day we shared with her. And the only way to recapture it in some measure was to bring a new puppy into our lives. By letting us know it would be better not to wait until Saturday to let her go, Annie gave us a push toward the future. It happened this way:

When Friday morning's edition of *The Washington Post* arrived, I went through the motions of leafing through the Weekend Section the way I always did (not that it was much of a distraction). In the Events Calendar for the weekend, I noticed a Corgi Fun Fair in nearby northern Virginia, scheduled for Saturday—which would be our first day without Annie.

We'd been to the previous year's Fun Fair and found ourselves at a delightful combination of dog show, picnic and circus. Instead of serious competition, Corgis and their people ran races and contests to decide which dogs had the biggest ears and which were the best kissers, among other events. If you've ever watched a dog show, I'll bet you've never seen anything like the contest where children tried to wrestle their Corgis into little doggie T-shirts.

I thought it might be good for us to go. For one thing, it would get us out of our suddenly all-too-empty house. And there's no better balm for a broken heart than watching a bunch of Corgis romping in a sunny field. In the back of my mind, I also hoped we might be able to make some connections that would lead us to one or two new puppies in the not-too-distant future.

But I didn't know how Susan would feel. So I didn't even mention it until Saturday morning. I was relieved to find that she also thought we should go.

It turned out to be a lovely day to spend Corgi-watching. We met some beautiful dogs and nice people. By asking where their dogs had come from, we found out about several highly-regarded breeders in Maryland and Pennsylvania. Two of them turned out to be next-door neighbors—and it was from those two breeders that we would soon get our new puppies, Mickey and Callie.

Had we waited until Saturday to say goodbye to Annie, we would not have gone to the Fun Fair. And we might not have found Mick and Cal. It was almost as if Annie had known what she had to do in order for us to move ahead with our lives. With her typical grace, she told us what we had to do, and gave us permission to fill the emptiness she left behind.

Before I formally introduce you to Mickey and Callie, there are a few more things I need to tell you about Annie.

Child-Friendly

A couple of months after Annie died, I went to my annual July Shore Leave STAR TREK convention near Baltimore. Annie had been such a fixture there for a decade, I knew people would ask me where she was when they saw me without her. I really didn't know if I'd be up to repeating dozens of times that she'd passed away. So I asked the convention committee if they'd mind replacing my photo in the program booklet with Annie's, and printing a little obituary under my bio. They said they'd be happy to oblige.

When I arrived at the hotel, I was surprised to find that the brief appreciation I'd written had been prominently printed inside the front cover. So all 1,500 *STAR TREK* fans at the convention got to see the dignified black and white picture of my pal, and these words:

IN MEMORIAM
MAIL ORDER ANNIE
6/7/81 TO 5/10/96

Howie and Susan are sad to report that they lost
their beloved Welsh Corgi companion Mail Order Annie
to cancer in May. Annie accompanied Howie to Maryland
STAR TREK conventions for most of her life. Fans were
always generous with their attention to Annie, and she
always enjoyed making her rounds. Annie even contributed
to charitable causes by offering "Ice Cream With Annie
(and Howie)" at auctions. Howie's favorite Annie convention
story recalls the time a tentative little girl approached them in
the hallway, wanting very much to pet Annie. But before she
did, she asked if Annie was "child-friendly."
She was indeed.
Annie was greatly loved. And she'll be greatly missed.

I was touched by the number of people who came up and told me how sorry they were to learn that Annie had died. A number of them recalled funny stories about Annie's convention appearances with me over the years. Some even wrote me notes and cards. But even more folks told me about their own beloved pets. And I really appreciated their kindness and willingness to share their own joy and grief with me.

Annie taught me...

Healing is easier when you don't have to do it alone.

Stars

During the time that Annie was sick, she had a special light to brighten her days—visits from a little neighbor, four-year-old Michele Wright, who lived across the street. Marc and Mary Ann, Michele's parents, had moved onto our brand-new block shortly before us, so we'd known Michele pretty much from the day she was born.

Right from the start, Michele was an enchanting child. With her big dark eyes, she observed everything, but she was in no hurry to talk. In fact, she barely spoke a word for her first two years. Yet she still managed to communicate pretty darned well. She reminded us a bit of Maggie, the silent, wide-and-wise-eyed baby with her omnipresent pacifier in the long-running animated TV sitcom, *THE SIMPSONS.*

Eventually, when she decided she had something she wanted to say, Michele started talking. But even in her silent days, she had a special bond with Annie. This gentle twinkling toddler and our Corgi lit up when they saw each other. Annie never walked past Michele's house without wanting to stop by and say hello. When Michele walked with us, she'd want to hold Annie's leash. Just as I'd done with my niece Kimberly ten years earlier, I would let Michele clutch the end of the leash in her little fist, and I'd hold the middle.

Once she knew Annie was sick, Michele came to see her as often as possible, bringing colorful pictures she'd drawn to cheer Annie up. One day, Michele proudly presented a gift she'd chosen herself at the pet store, a little hot-pink squeaky dragon. By then, Annie was too tired to play with it, so Michele placed it on a low bookshelf where Annie could see it from her pillow and blankets.

When Annie died, we were afraid to tell Michele. We had no idea how she'd react. How do four-year-olds conceptualize death? What does it mean to them? As far as we knew, Annie was the first living thing Michele had loved and lost. Fortunately, she took it in stride. She knew we were sad, and she knew she'd never see Annie again. But she said she would always remember Annie.

Later that year, Michele and her parents spent some vacation time at the beach. When they came back, Mary Ann told us something that happened on their trip. One night, while she and her parents were out looking at the clear night sky, Michele announced, "The stars are Annie's footprints going to heaven."

We were glad that our amazing little dog and amazing little Michele had the good fortune to know and love each other.

Life After Annie:
Meeting Mickey & Callie

Susan and I decided to add a pair of puppies to our lives. And we wanted them to become best friends, the way Annie and Hawkeye had. So we wanted to find two different breeders from whom we would get one puppy each, and bring them home a day or two apart. That way, whichever puppy arrived first wouldn't have enough time to stake any kind of possessive claim over territory—or us!

But Mickey upended our plans.

We'd learned of several well-regarded breeders during our trip to the Corgi Fun Fair, including the two living next door to each other in Landenberg, Pennsylvania. Landenberg is a little town in farm country outside of Philadelphia. As we learned on our first visit, Landenberg seems to be something of a mushroom-growing mecca. I have no idea why. It didn't seem any darker or damper there than anywhere else.

The two next-door breeders were Susan Strickland and Lois Kay. Both had just welcomed litters of puppies, which would be available at roughly the same time during mid-summer. So we made plans to visit both breeders on the Saturday of Memorial Day weekend, two weeks after Annie had crossed the legendary Rainbow Bridge to doggie heaven.

It just so happened that my parents decided to come down from New York to visit us the same weekend. So we all piled into my Honda station wagon and took the two-hour drive to Landenberg.

Our first appointment was with Lois Kay at Terenelf Kennels. Lois welcomed us to her home and asked us questions, but we never felt like we were being interrogated. We brought along pictures of Annie and told Lois all about her. We met some of Lois's beautiful, friendly dogs.

Michele goofs around with her new puppy pals

Then we went back out to the porch, and she brought out a four-month-old female bearing the dignified, ethereal name of Terenelf's Heavenly Stars, with the more manageable but still delicate call-name of Heather.

Those names, to put it mildly, did not match the furry fireball that exploded out of the house. She was as far from dignified and dainty as you can get. Instead, she was silly and goofy and free-spirited. She'd been trained not at all, and had lived her first four months coming and going as she pleased. A true wild child.

She immediately took great delight in herding my mother to the corner of the porch and untying any and all shoelaces within her reach. Little Heavenly Stars had been fathered by Patrick, one of the most handsome and sought-after stud dogs in the area. We had coincidentally met several of Patrick's offspring at the Corgi Fun Fair, and they were all beautiful and sweet-tempered. And we'd actually made an effort to obtain a Patrick puppy directly from his breeder, Gigi Fitzgerald, only to find that none were currently available.

But that was about to change.

Puppy Mickey makes a new friend on our block

After we played with this shooting star of a puppy for a while, Lois told us she'd been planning to keep her as a potential show dog. But now she suspected the pup would end up too small for the show circuit. If we were interested in her, Lois would be willing to sell her to us.

We were stunned. We weren't expecting to get a puppy this quickly. Annie's bed was barely cold! And what about our plans to get two puppies at the same time?

Still, this puppy was adorable. And plans are made to be changed, after all. Was there any reason not to take Miss Heavenly Stars? We asked for a couple of days to think it over, which Lois was more than happy to grant. If we decided we wanted this puppy, we could come back to get her on Memorial Day Monday, after my parents had gone home. We'd let Lois know as soon as we'd made up our minds.

In a slight daze after our unexpected possible good fortune at Lois Kay's house, we went to Susan Strickland's Honeyfox Kennel. The litter from which we might choose our second puppy had been born less than four weeks earlier, so they were still in their little nursery pen with momma Sally.

After passing mutual inspection, Susan Strickland brought us in to meet Sally and her eight babies, all sisters. I'd never seen puppies so young before. And when we came in, it was mealtime. With long-suffering forbearance, Sally rested on her side while the pups suckled. She wore the saintly but harried expression common to new mothers of many species. And when she decided mealtime was over, and she got up to get away for a break, one puppy refused to let go. Seeing this baby Corgi hanging on for every last gulp was quite a sight.

At that age, puppies look like generic little furballs, since they haven't taken on breed-specific characteristics yet. Some of Sally's tiny children teetered on unsteady legs, having had only limited experience with the miracle of locomotion. Others huddled together for warmth and comfort. I wish we'd taken pictures that day, so we might have been able to pick out later which puppy would become our Callie.

Susan and Mickey

We concluded our visit by telling Susan Strickland we would indeed like one of Sally's puppies, and we left a token reservation deposit. In a month, we'd come back to choose the one we wanted.

(For more on finding a top-notch breeder and picking a puppy, see the appropriate sections just ahead in **Book Two**.)

Bringing Mickey Home

Susan and I decided to take Heavenly Stars. But neither that name nor Heather seemed suitable. Susan couldn't think of anything. Then I came up with an idea. I've been a baseball fan since I was seven. A die-hard, true-blue New York Yankees fan, to be specific. When I was growing up, the legendary Mickey Mantle was my favorite player. (Yeah, me and several million other kids of my generation.)

Mantle, who'd played hard and lived harder, ended up with liver cancer. After a highly publicized transplant, The Mick had died the year before. Since cancer had also claimed Annie, I thought it would be a nice way to pay homage to both Annie and my boyhood baseball idol by naming our puppy after him. Susan had no objections, so Heather became Mickey.

Picking Callie

A few weeks after Mickey came to live with us, we bundled her in the car and took our next trip to Landenberg. We figured as long as we were there, we could pay a call on Lois and leave Mickey to visit with her relatives while we went next door to Susan Strickland's to choose Mickey's adopted sister-to-be.

By this time, most of Sally's babies had been spoken for. So we sat on the floor to play with the two remaining unchosen. One was a typical playful puppy. But the other was... *unusual*. First, her coloring was unique; she had much more white on her face than the typical Corgi. Her eyes were almost black, also unusual for a Corgi. And the dark pigmentation around her eyes (commonly called "mascara") was wider than the norm, which made her eyes look *enormous*.

This dark-eyed baby wasn't shy, exactly. But she was reserved and deliberate in everything she did, with none of the endearing silliness common to almost every puppy. She was a puppy of a different color, in more ways than one.

In particular, she wanted this long furry boa toy that her sister was happily dragging around the kitchen. Remember that most seven or eight-week-old puppies have very short attention spans. Not little Dark-eyes. She let us play with her and hold her and pet her. But she never stopped watching her sister and the boa. The moment

Callie liberates the prized snake-toy from her less-attentive sister

her sister dropped the boa, Dark-eyes circled around, grabbed it and carried it off to a far corner—continuing to keep a wary eye on her sister.

Well, this studious little waif was the total opposite of happy, goofy Mickey—and she captured our hearts. She was the one, and we'd come back to get her in two weeks.

But what to name her? Susan and I were stumped. Nothing seemed to fit. We began to think we'd have a puppy with no name at all. Then, one day, we were in a bookstore at the mall. And we decided to do a little spontaneous research. Since Corgis originally hailed from Wales, we decided to delve into Celtic folklore and see if we could come up with something appropriate.

After a while, we found an entry describing an obscure and ancient goddess of the moon and the hunt, known as Callie Berry. And that's what we decided to call her. The perfect name had been there all along, just waiting for us to discover it.

Little did we know how *cosmically* perfect the name would truly be. That realization did not come together until much later, when it dawned on us that we'd been part of circumstances so inexplicable that I wouldn't have believed them—if I hadn't *known* for a fact they were *true*.

Sunbeam & Moonbeam

So. Do you believe in fate? I don't know if I do. But I do know the baffling sequence inextricably linking Annie and Callie. Remember the mystical night when we heard those ghostly notes from the music box?

The early hours of May First.

The night Annie almost left us.

Also: the date a litter of eight female Corgis came into the world at Honeyfox Kennel.

And: the advent of a full moon.

Susan makes Callie feel at home

Yet, the conjunction of these events did not occur to us until months later. Months after we happened to choose to name our second new puppy after a Celtic moon goddess without realizing the auspicious portents attending the day of her birth. In retrospect, our choice of name could not have been more fitting if it been pre-ordained.

And maybe it was.

As Callie grew up, she seemed to take on many of Annie's character traits and behavioral preferences. The older she gets, the more this happens. It's really quite uncanny. And we couldn't help wondering: Poets and writers have long imagined that strange things happen under the moon's bewitching influence. Is it possible that Annie and Callie touched spirits in the full moon's cool silver light that May night? I'd like to think they did.

And it was altogether natural for Susan, who had called Annie "Sunbeam," to start calling Callie her "Moonbeam."

Annie's Legacy

I mentioned earlier how Annie's final gift to me and Susan had been her permission to let her go and to enter the next phase of our lives, with new puppies to love, and to love us. She also bequeathed a great gift to Mickey and Callie. Thanks to Annie's enduring and cheerful tutelage, I was a much more patient and prepared puppy-parent the second time around. And Mickey and Callie benefitted from all the things Annie taught me about dogs—and about myself.

Mickey and Callie are both four years old as I write this. I've tried to remember to take greater joy in their formative years and to fret less than I did with Annie. Annie taught me that. And I allow myself to treasure the time we spend together, because I know now how swiftly the years of a dog's life pass. Annie's spirit is always here to remind me of those things.

And I carry with me Annie's greatest lesson. The superlative old Broadway musical *DAMN YANKEES* has a showstopping tune called "You've Gotta Have Heart." My dictionary defines that use of the word *heart* as "*courage and enthusiasm.*" Well, Annie had more heart than anyone I've ever known, human or otherwise. I wish I could be more like her.

And yet, as much as Annie taught me, Mickey and Callie seem to understand I still have things to learn. In their own unique ways, they're doing their best to continue my education.

Sweet, jubilant Mickey teaches me the value of love and forgiveness in the way she greets as a friend everyone she meets. She's so innocent, she reminds us of the little red Elmo character from *SESAME STREET*. It never dawns on Mickey that anyone could possibly *not* love her, that anyone would not be happy to see her little smiling face.

Mickey (top) and Callie take turns under the couch

And what a million-watt smile Mickey has! We call her the Julia Roberts of Corgis: when her smile lights her beautiful face, you can't help but smile back. I could do much worse than to emulate the cheerful way she bounds through life.

This past summer, I was invited to talk about dogs and training to a "Nature & Animals" class offered as part of Howard Community College's excellent "Kids on Campus" program. Mickey went with me, and we spent over an hour sitting on the floor with a dozen eager 9-year-olds brimming with questions. For Mickey, being surrounded by kids wanting to pet her and see her tricks was nothing short of Paradise.

Meanwhile, winsome, shy Callie teaches me about determination and intensity in the way she makes certain I don't forget to feed her, and the take-no-prisoners way she plays ball. She flies through the air with fearless grace, and lets nothing get in her way. I wish I could pursue my goals with such fierceness. But she also stops to roll gleefully on her back, and understands the spiritual necessity of taking a belly-rub break when the mood strikes her.

On her vet visits, Callie is still the studious little waif we met in Susan Strickland's kitchen. Up on the exam table, she'll observe everything the tech and doctor do to examine and treat her. She walks to the end of the table to watch them type data into the computer. She stands on the paper chart, reading as they write notes. She takes me to the lab to watch the doctor examine a slide. And when we leave, she stops in behind the front desk to watch the receptionists at work.

And if we had any doubts that Callie is truly enchanted, well, this is a dog who *never* gets dirty and *always* smells like flowers and baby powder. Proof positive: one spring afternoon, a gorgeous black and purple butterfly alighted on Callie's back, drawn by the unerring instinct that brings butterflies to blossoms. Except that this time, the blossom was a little furrier than usual.

As I've worked on this book, writing late into the afternoons, Mickey and Callie often come up and rest on the floor next to my chair, much as Annie used to do. They're within easy reach, and I take advantage of the joyous opportunities to scratch their velvet-soft ears and furry pink bellies. Then, Callie in particular will give me a look, reminding me—again, much as Annie would—that it is considerably *past* time for dogs to have their dinner.

I know now that it's not disloyal get a new dog when a beloved old dog dies. And I have a confession, now safe to make: I was afraid I'd never be able to love new puppies as much as I loved Annie. It took some time to tame that fear, but Mickey and Callie waited for me to come around.

Having Mickey and Callie isn't *exact*ly like having Annie. Individual dogs are as different from each other as are people.

Changing of the guard:
Cal and Mick use Annie's bench
for their daily "Mommy-Watch"

But there's continuity.

And I take comfort in knowing that Callie and Mickey get to enjoy the fruits of all the things that Annie taught me about dogs... and about people.

I'm a better person because Annie was such a great dog.

And, right this moment, I'm a better person who'd better go feed his very hungry Corgis. Thanks for sharing Annie's life with me.

Callie in her favorite place: mommy's embrace

Oh... one other thing. Would you do me a little favor? If you have a pet (any pet), go give your buddy a little extra love. Our pets deserve it. Tell 'em Annie sent you. You'll feel better for it. And you'll be better for it, too.

Annie taught me that.

End of Book One

🐾

Book Two

"Teach Your
Puppy Well"

Puppy Prep 101

To have the best chance of navigating successfully through the first days and weeks of puppyhood with your new pal, it pays to be prepared. In this section, we'll talk about what you need to know—and what you should have on hand—before you bring a puppy or dog home to live with you.

Is a Dog the Right Pet for You?
12 Key Questions...

Since you're reading this book, we'll assume you *have* decided a dog is indeed the right pet for you. But—just to be on the safe side—here are a few questions you'll want to ask yourself (and answer honestly) before you take the next step and actually get a dog.

1. Am I ready, willing and able to put in the time it takes to care for and train a puppy or dog?

2. Am I willing to commit to this little creature for the next 10 or 15 years, come what may? (Dogs should be no more disposable than children!)

3. Am I committed enough to deal with inevitable trouble, problems and inconvenience?

4. Do I understand that it may take two years of on-going efforts to properly train a puppy?

5. Do I understand that my life will revolve around a puppy's needs and training for much of those two years—and to a lesser extent for the rest of my dog's life?

6. Do I understand that it's unfair to keep a puppy confined for the entire workday of 8 to 12 hours?

7. Can I get home to take my puppy out for a mid-day potty walk?

8. If not, can I make other arrangements?

9. Do I have time to take my dogs for regular walks every day, weather permitting?

10. Can I afford the expenses of caring for a dog?

11. If I live in an apartment, does the management allow dogs?

12. Do I understand that it's not okay to tie a dog out in the yard or garage, or lock him in the basement whenever he "gets in the way" of something else going on?

If you can *honestly* answer "yes" to all these questions, then by all means forge ahead and get a dog.

But if you have doubts, then please think long and hard before you make this decision.

Dogs are great pets and companions, but they don't fit every lifestyle. For instance, if you work long hours, like to spend many of your evenings out on the town, or tend to travel often—to places and by modes of transport that make it impossible to take your dog with you—then getting a dog may not be the best choice for you.

Dogs are pack animals. They don't thrive when forced to spend most of their time alone. There are quite a few similarities between having a dog and having a child. Both require considerable time, energy, supervision, patience, education and attention on a continuing basis.

I'm *not* equating the two—there are obvious differences between being a parent and having a dog, including (but not limited to) these facts: your dog will *never* ask for the car keys; and you *won't* have to send him college. And you *can* leave your puppy home alone in his crate for four hours without ending up on the evening news when the authorities descend on you for neglecting your "offspring."

But when I meet with training clients who are young, as-yet-childless couples, there are sufficient similarities for me to mention that their puppy is, in essence, a "practice kid." I don't know of any statistics to support this, but I'd be willing to bet that the lessons learned from raising a puppy first can be helpful in preparing first-time parents for the trials—and joys—of having a human baby join the "pack."

And I've had a number of clients who already have kids comment on the similarities between puppy-care and child-care strategies.

Still, there are an astounding number of people who make ill-considered decisions when it comes to getting a dog. So please do yourself—and some innocent pup—a favor: *being sure is much better than being sorry.*

Picking a Pal: Best Dogs for You

Purebreed or mixed breed? Puppy or adult dog? Male or female? Big or little? Long coat or short?

If you already have your pup, or you know where you'll be getting her, you can skip ahead to **Choosing A Vet** or **Stuff to Buy**. But if not, then you may be pondering these very choices. Making the wrong choices can make a huge difference in how much you and your dog enjoy life together. So how will you decide?

Mickey, the "Julia Roberts of Corgis," shows off her star quality

Confession: there are entire books written on this issue. You may want to pick up one of those books at the library or bookstore, to supplement what we cover here. But, right now, let's summarize the major questions involved in this decision.·

First and foremost:

🐾 Please DON'T get a dog on impulse.

🐾 Don't let your kids, your heart, or the seller browbeat you into a snap decision.

Purebreed or Mixed Breed?

Whether descended from champions or possessed of a "Heinz 57" pedigree of unknown origin, almost any dog has the potential to be a great companion and pet.

A purebreed dog should have predictable characteristics. If you buy a well-bred Golden Retriever puppy, you should have a fair idea of how big she'll get and what her personality may be like.

With mixed-breed pups, even if you know the ingredients (say, a Lab/Beagle), it's hard to know which breed characteristics will be dominant. So there may be no way to predict whether a Lab-Beagle will grow up to weigh 20 pounds or 80 pounds.

- Mixed breeds cost less. They may even be free!
- For a purebred pup, be prepared to pay $500 and up—in some cases, *way up*! The most expensive purebred pups are what breeders call "show quality," meaning they appear to have physical characteristics that meet the highest standards of that particular breed.

135

- Other pups from the same litter may have some physical imper-fections (for example: stance, teeth, coat, shape of eyes or ears) that make them less desirable as show dogs. These "pet quali-ty" pups may cost slightly less.

- If your budget is limited—and don't forget that initial purchase price is just a fraction of first-year pup-related expenses—then a mixed breed may be the dog for you.

- On the other hand, if money is no object, and you have your heart set on a particular kind of dog, then open your wallet and follow your heart.

Which Breed?

There are well over 125 recognized dog breeds, ranging from the popular (Labs and Goldens) to the exotic (Komondor and Kavasz, to name just two—and only from the K's). With so many choices, does it matter which one you pick? *Yes!*

Within a margin of variability, well-bred individuals of any given breed should have predictable physical and temperamental characteristics. This gives you the chance to choose a breed that's right for you.

The main advantage of choosing a purebreed dog is that you have some idea what you're getting before you bring a puppy home.

If you're a couch potato, does it make sense to pick a breed that needs lots of exercise? On the other hand, if you plan to take your dog jogging with you every morning, don't get a short-legged, slow-moving Basset Hound. If you have small, high-spirited children, don't get a fragile, nerv-ous breed. If you choose a breed compatible with your lifestyle and per-sonality, you'll be less likely to face a doggie divorce later.

A bit of research will help narrow down the choices. Breed books are a good introductory source of facts, and eagerly herald the sterling quali-ties of their subjects. However, they may hesitate to say anything remote-ly negative about the breed they're written to promote.

A great way to find out about a particular breed: talk to the people who breed them. Many breeders will give you the straight scoop on their dogs, pro and con.

And a great way to meet breeders: go to dog shows in your area. If you can't get there first thing in the morning, try to find out the schedule ahead of time. If you're interested in Collies, and you arrive hours after the last Collie has left the ring, you may find that all the Collie breeders have packed up and gone home. Since the purpose of your visit is to talk to breeders about their dogs, this won't help you.

When you get to the show arena, locate the corner where the Collies are hanging out. Most dog people are happy to talk to prospective owners (assuming they're not frantically grooming a dog who's due in the ring in ten seconds). Ask honest questions, and you're likely to get honest answers.

Talk to a Collie breeder and you'll find someone who loves Collies, who wants you to love Collies, too—but who also wants you to get a Collie only if Lassie is the right breed for you. Breeders have a vested interest in the healthy promotion of their special breed—an interest not served by having someone buy a Collie and end up unhappy with that choice.

Check out the internet. Many breed clubs have web sites, which may include calendars of breed shows and events, in addition to basic information on the dogs themselves. The American Kennel Club, the major purebreed sanctioning group in the United States, has a web site (www.akc.org) from which you can link to many breed-specific clubs and web sites.

Puppy vs. Older Dog

Having a puppy is a lot like having a 2-year-old human toddler. Both are amazingly speedy and curious, capable of getting into major trouble in no time at all. Both require constant supervision, patience and education. Not everyone has the energy or time to deal with a puppy's needs.

- Puppies can have seemingly boundless energy.
- Puppies need to be housebroken.
- Puppies will chew on anything and everything.
- It may take two years of consistent work and positive reinforcement for puppies to become well-trained, adult dogs.
- Older dogs may be easier to housebreak—they may already *be* housebroken.
- Older dogs have longer attention spans, so they may learn new things more quickly.
- On the other hand, older dogs may have acquired bad habits that need to be changed through obedience training.
- Older dogs still need exercise. But they generally have less energy than young puppies.

So there's no right or wrong answer to this question. The choice depends on you. I often see shell-shocked clients who whimper: "I had *no idea* puppies were this much work!"

If you're prepared for what it takes to raise a puppy, then you're likely to survive the process and succeed with flying colors. But if you do your homework, and you don't think you have the time or energy for a puppy, then perhaps an older dog is the pet for you.

Big vs. Little

Puppies grow up. Some more than others.

Golden Retriever or Lab pups weighing 20 pounds at two months will likely be up to 40 or 50 pounds by six months. Many new pup-owners are not prepared for how quickly their tiny fluffballs grow big and strong. And big-breed pups may continue to gain weight well into their second year.

A 10-pound Welsh Corgi pup, by contrast, reaches her full weight of 25 pounds by the time she's a year old.

- Pound for pound, dogs are much stronger than humans. How much dog are you prepared to handle? If you're a 110 pound woman, you might want to think twice about getting a dog that can effortlessly drag you down the street. But if you start training that big-breed puppy immediately, you may never have a problem controlling a dog that outweighs you.
- Big dogs eat lots more. And more food costs more money.
- And more going in *one* end means more coming *out* the other.
- Big dogs take up more space in your home or car. So do their crates.
- Big puppies who have yet to learn good manners are more likely to knock down and scare small children.
- Small dogs may have to be protected from rough-playing children.
- Big dogs have more hair to shed. They take longer to groom.

None of these factors should necessarily rule out a big dog or a small one. They're just things for you to think about.

Male vs. Female

Male dogs are usually larger.

Unless you know what you're doing, nobody should breed a dog just for the fun of it. It's not fun—taking care of a litter of helpless puppies is a lot of work and expense. You will not get rich selling puppies. And only the best physical specimens with the best temperaments should reproduce. So most of us should exercise effective doggie birth control. It costs more to spay a female than to neuter a male.

Personally, I prefer female potty habits. A female dog goes to her spot and empties her bladder. Male dogs like to stroll down the street, scent-marking on every tree, post and stop sign.

Some experts say that male dogs may be more aggressive or dominant. But timely spaying or neutering often heads off aggression problems before they begin. And both genders are equally teachable.

Best Places to Get a Dog

Breeders

The best place to get a purebred puppy is from a "reputable" breeder. Look for a breeder who:

- breeds carefully, taking genetics into account
- breeds for temperament as well as physical features
- breeds several female dogs and doesn't breed the same mother over and over
- has clean kennels and puppy "nursery" areas
- has healthy-looking dogs with good personalities
- doesn't breed parent dogs with undesirable traits
- doesn't sell a puppy to just anyone
- answers questions and gives information on care and feeding
- gives you a good feeling (this is subjective)
- loves her dogs and doesn't breed them only for profit
- doesn't pressure you into making a rushed decision

A reputable breeder prefers to interview prospective owners to assure that they're a good match for the breed and have a good grasp of how to care for a new pup. You'll do better by buying from a breeder who cares where her pups go.

Lois Kay, from whom we got Mickey, is an exceptional example of the best kind of breeder. Not only does she care who gets her pups, she even holds occasional "open house" parties at her Terenelf Kennel, where she invites prospective buyers to watch and participate in puppy evaluations.

Finding Good Breeders

- ❧ Contact the American Kennel Club (either on their web site or by calling 919-233-9767) to get information on local or regional breed clubs in your area.

- ❧ Breed clubs maintain lists of breeders.

- ❧ Go to local dog shows, talk to breeders, get referrals

Once you've decided on a particular breed, it's a good idea to locate a few breeders within a 2-hour drive of home. Ideally, you should try to make 2 or 3 visits. First visit, you'll get acquainted and meet the breeder's other dogs.

Make your second visit when the puppies are 6 or 7 weeks old to choose yours from the group. On the third visit, you'll actually take your 8-or-9-week-old puppy home.

In some cases, of course, you'll choose a puppy on your first visit. Find out ahead of time if the puppies are old enough to leave for their new homes. If the timing is right, *be prepared*. Take a crate with you, and have what you need ready at home. (See **Stuff to Buy** on page 151.)

Try to avoid buying a puppy sight unseen. I'd also shy away from breeders located too far away to visit on a comfortable day trip by car.

Warning Signs: Buyer Beware!

- ❧ Avoid "back-yard breeders"—folks who think it might be fun to breed their dog once or twice. They may mean well, but breeding is a science and should be done carefully. Inexperienced breeders may be unprepared for all the time and expense involved in caring for newborn pups, and they may skip vital medical care.

- ❧ Roadside signs that say "Puppies for sale" are tempting. But drive on by. The best breeders have no need to advertise in this way: they find buyers by referral, and usually have waiting lists for puppies.

- ❧ Same for newspaper ads. Reputable breeders don't seek buyers with mass-market ads. They want to be selective about who gets their pups—and you should be selective about where you go to buy a pup.

- ❧ Papers—Don't be impressed by ads that brag about "AKC Registered Pups" or "pups with papers." Pedigree documents may be worth less than the paper they're printed on if you don't know anything about the breeder or her dogs.

Picking and buying a puppy is stressful enough without putting yourself in a situation where you feel like: "If I'm driving eight hours, I *will* come back with a *puppy!*"

I've also had clients who located puppies via the internet, requiring long trips to purchase a pooch under shadowy circumstances. Not the best way to go about getting a dog.

Most breeds can be obtained from good breeders closer to home. It's worth keeping that in mind. And be flexible: don't lock yourself into an impossible time-frame for obtaining a puppy that can only be met by getting one from halfway across the country.

Breed Rescue Groups

Many breed clubs have "rescue" operations. Their goal is to keep their favorite dogs from ending up at animal shelters. Here's how they work. Say Joe owns a Golden Retriever, but his job is sending him overseas and he can't take his beloved Daisy with him.

But Joe doesn't want to take Daisy to the local shelter and cast his dog's fate to the winds. He wants to know that Daisy will find a good home.

So Joe calls his local Golden Retriever club. The volunteer in charge of rescues calls him back and finds out all about Daisy. If the rescue group knows of a suitable home, arrangements will be made and Daisy will go to her new family. If a new home is not immediately available, Daisy may spend some time with a foster family.

A rescue is not a monetary transaction. Joe gets no payment for Daisy, just the knowledge that his dog will be well-cared-for by a new owner who really wants her.

Rescue dogs may be puppies, young adults or older dogs. And many of them are up for adoption not because they were "problem" dogs, but only because their owners' circumstances changed in a way that prevented them from keeping their pets. In some cases, dogs come to rescue groups because their previous owners become ill or die.

If you want a particular breed—and the idea of taking in a homeless dog appeals to you—then a rescue dog may be the pet for you. Since rescue groups are run by volunteers, you may have to pay a fee of some kind to help defray the expenses involved. But it will certainly be far less than the cost of buying a purebreed puppy.

So adopting a rescue dog may give you a way to get a purebred pet, even if your budget is limited.

Animal Shelters

Another way to do a good deed and adopt a dog in need, of course, is to go to your local animal shelter. Once known as "the pound," where ill-fated animals were destroyed after a few miserable days in a dirty cage, today's shelters are just as likely to be clean, well-lit way-stations for stray or surrendered animals.

In addition to the municipal shelters in many areas, you may also live near a private non-profit shelter. The most enlightened (and best-funded) shelters try not to destroy any animal that seems a good adoption candidate.

CAUTION: don't let your heart over-rule your head. It's easy to walk through a shelter and fall in love with a poor needy pooch. But once again, don't make an impulsive decision. Think about whether that pup is the right one for you, your family and your circumstances.

Take the time to play with any dogs who appeal to you. Bring a few treats. Come back a second time, and confirm your first impression. Better to lose out on a dog you wanted than to rush into something and regret it. Better for both you and the dog.

Fortunately, many shelters require a detailed application, plus an interview by a staff member or volunteer trained in placement evaluation. The best shelters also send someone to check out your home environment. While some consider all this inconvenient and onerous, it's best for both people and pets. The last thing shelters want is failed adoptions and returned animals.

Many animal advocates devote considerable energy to promotion of shelter adoption. And they should be saluted for doing so. A second chance may be all a dog needs to become a great pet.

Still, what I'm about to say *needs* to be said:

Adopting a shelter dog may present a unique set of challenges.

Some dogs at shelters have previously been neglected or abused. They may have been owned by people too busy, ignorant or clueless to know—or to find out—how to properly take care of a puppy or dog. And dogs of any age can be negatively affected by improper socialization and care.

- Neglected dogs often receive little or no training—and may have been allowed to develop negative habits.
- You'll have to deal with those by replacing them with positive behaviors.
- It may be impossible for shelter staff to guess how long a stray has been on its own. Stressed-out strays may need lots of TLC.

- If a dog's history is unknown, it's not always possible to predict how he may adapt to a new home.

None of these factors should scare you away from considering shelter adoption. A responsible shelter will not even try to place dogs with major behavioral problems. And they'll inform prospective owners of smaller potential problems.

For a reasonable fee, many trainers will be happy to help you evaluate a shelter pup early in the adoption process. A professional eye may notice things—both positive and negative—that you may not.

Even if you go ahead without the advice of a trainer, it's a good idea to meet with a trainer soon after bringing your adopted pet home. If you get a puppy, you'll want to begin basic obedience education right away. One or two private sessions with a trainer can get you started on the right foot. Or you can join a group class. But it helps to have the guidance of someone with experience in teaching all kinds of puppies from all different backgrounds.

If you get an adult dog, you may find he's already had some education in the social graces that make pups into good pets. A trainer can help you figure out what your new pal already knows, and what he still needs to learn.

Humble beginnings do not preclude greatness. So your amazing companion may be waiting for you at the nearest animal shelter. If you go in prepared to make a rational, informed choice, you may come out with the pet of your dreams.

Picking a Puppy

Say you've decided to get a young puppy. Are there things you should know before choosing one from all those cute, squirmy little furballs? Yes.

Are so-called "puppy tests" foolproof? No. Dr. Nicholas Dodman, director of the Behavior Clinic at Tufts University School of Veterinary Medicine, believes "the jury is still out on the predictive value" of puppy temperament tests, typically given at 7 or 8 weeks of age. However, Dr. Dodman also says these tests may help you to predict behavioral extremes—excessive dominance at one end of the spectrum or shyness at the other.

So, what should you look for in a puppy (or older dog, for that matter)?

POSITIVE TRAITS	NEGATIVE TRAITS
• Outgoing • Friendly • Curious • Attentive • Playful • Responsive to food-treats (like a piece of cheese) • Reasonably willing to accept restraint • Willing to be petted	• Very shy • Very dominant • Very mouthy and nippy • Fearful • Excessively reactive to stimuli (like noise) • Unwilling to be petted • Unwilling to be restrained

In his fascinating book *The Intelligence of Dogs*, psychologist/trainer Stanley Coren describes 12 Obedience Personality Tests and a scoring system. Here's a sampling of the Coren tests:

- **Attraction**: Sit or crouch on the floor. Using a cheerful voice (calling "Puppy! Puppy!") and some hand-claps, try to get the pup to approach you. Then slowly stand, and as you back away, try to get her to follow you a bit. Look for a pup that's curious and attentive. Skip the aggressive or fearful pup. Skip the pup who ignores you.

- **Dominance**: Gently turn a pup on her back and hold her there. Don't wrestle, just be gentle but firm. Skip the pup who fights like her life depends on it, scratching, growling and biting—she may have a hard time accepting you as pack leader. Also skip the pup who just lies there with no reaction at all. This is a submissive position; the ideal pup *should* protest a bit. But then she should settle down, at which point you can reward her with a little tummy rub, then let her up.

- **Petting**: Puppies should enjoy petting and "skritches," especially under the chin, on the chest, behind the ears. For the moment, avoid petting directly on top of the head if it's a pup you're just meeting. Some pups consider that a challenge. Skip the pups who try to bite your hand every time it comes close—also skip the ones who seem afraid or very shy.

- **Reaction to Noise**: When the puppy isn't watching you, try clapping your hands sharply, rattling a soda can with some pennies inside, or jingling a loud set of keys. Ideal pups react quickly and with some interest, but without fear or excessive barking.

Remember: these tests can't tell you *absolutely* what a puppy will be like when she grows up. They *may* help you avoid a difficult pup. But as with humans, a dog's eventual personality is influenced both by genetics and environment. Two aspects of puppy behavior are out of your control: biology, and how they're raised in their first few crucial weeks of life. But you do have control over which puppy you pick, and what you do to train her after she comes home to be your pet.

Don't expect to find a perfect pup. Do look for a pup somewhere in the middle on those puppy tests. Choose wisely—start training right away—and you'll have a good chance to raise a great puppy.

For Parents: Kids & Dogs

For generations, sharing childhood with a family dog has been part of growing up. It still is today, but the misty images of bygone decades don't match up with big changes in family structure—in families with both parents working, and in single-parent households, adults simply don't have as much time to take care of a dog these days.

Still, many parents really want to give their kids the experience of having a beloved pet and companion. And kids become experts at lobbying to convince mom and/or dad to get a dog.

Many of my training clients are families, of all shapes and sizes. And it's worth pointing out some of the pitfalls to other parents who may be considering (or may have just purchased) a dog or puppy.

A puppy is a lot like adding a 2-year-old toddler to the family—*a very fast toddler with very sharp teeth.*

An older dog is more akin to a 5-year-old human child: able to be taught and trusted—up to a point—but still in need of supervision and attention.

Most children and most puppies won't intentionally hurt each other. But puppies jump and nip as part of their natural play, until they're taught not to. Sharp puppy teeth hurt. And smaller children can be terrorized by playful puppies. As a result, even the best behaved child may hit or kick a puppy out of fear. So what can parents do to keep everybody safe?

- A parent should be present when kids play with young, untrained puppies—ready to intervene at a moment's notice to keep things under control. Using a leash helps.

- Younger kids need to be protected from over-exuberant puppies. And puppies need to be protected from children who may grab ears and tails, poke eyes, step on toes, or fall on small furry bodies.

- Only a parent can keep kids and pups from competing for toys. If kids leave their toys all over the family room floor, the puppy is going to grab them—especially if they resemble dog toys. One solution: separate toy boxes. Many children can be motivated to put their toys away if they don't want the puppy to chew on them.

- Older children (7 and up, depending on maturity) can take part in puppy training sessions. When you practice pup-school lessons at home, teach kids how to teach pups. This accomplishes 2 things: it makes kids feel less helpless, and it helps pups understand that even small humans may be authority figures. Dogs are very good at discerning pack-order and living by pack rules.

How much can you reasonably expect of children when it comes to contributing to puppy care? Well, every child is different. But I've heard many parents say something like, "When *we* agreed to get this puppy, *you* agreed to help take care of him."

I don't know about you, but I seem to remember times when I'd agree to almost *anything* in order to get what I wanted. Kids still do that, don't they?

But lots of *grown-ups* are unprepared for how much time and work puppy-care requires—is it fair to expect *kids* to shoulder a large part of the burden? Probably not .

Should kids pitch in? *Absolutely.* Children 10 and up can be trusted to take pups out for walks. And they're old enough to poop-scoop, too—no matter how much they make faces and moan, "It's *gross*! It's *squishy*! It's *warm*!" I've heard all those and more. Picking up solid poops in a plastic bag is something most kids can master (though it's probably easier to deal with soft, runny poops yourself).

But kids deserve time to be kids. They need to be with their friends, do homework, crash in front of the TV set, play computer games... *kid stuff.*

- Having *realistic* pup-care expectations of children may indeed teach valuable lessons in responsibility.

- Having *unrealistic* expectations, however, may end up doing the opposite: teaching kids to give up in the face of a tough task.

Another thing to consider: if the *kids* are shirking pup-care work, and the *parents* refuse to do what the kids swore they'd do, then *nobody's* taking proper care of the dog. And that's not fair to the dog. This all-too-common situation virtually guarantees failure.

Here are a few ways to make success more likely:

- Before getting a dog, parents can make sure older children have a clear idea of how much work it is to have a puppy.
- Draw up a list of pup-care jobs. Let your kids pick some tasks which will become their responsibility.
- But make sure these are things your kids can realistically do. Don't expect a 40-pound child to walk a 50-pound Labrador puppy. But that same child can certainly feed the puppy.
- Write up a contract to be signed by your kids. Make sure they understand they'll be expected to do these jobs *all* the time, not only when they feel like it.
- Accept the fact that the actuality of having a puppy may require some contract re-negotiation later on.
- Remember the *main goal*: to successfully raise a puppy and add a wonderful companion to your family—*not* to contribute to a miserable failure you and your kids will regret for the rest of your lives.
- *Be flexible.* The potential rewards are more than worth it.

Choosing a Veterinarian

Before you bring your new pooch home, you should have a veterinarian picked out. No matter where you get your pet, you'll want to bring her in for a general check-up within a day or two. Most pups are healthy—but you'll want to be sure there are no medical problems needing immediate care.

One of my neighbors got a puppy as a surprise pre-Christmas gift. When she brought him over to show him off, the little guy had a cough and seemed listless. I got her an appointment to see my vet that very day, before the long holiday weekend (when offices would be closed). It turned out her pup had pneumonia—serious but treatable, as long as it was dealt with right away.

Seeing a vet quickly also means your pup will start a medical history and get on the proper schedule for all recommended care, including inoculations.

Today's vets are modern versions of the ol' country-doc general practitioner. The best of them are multi-talented clinicians, diagnosticians, surgeons, dentists and students of psychology (both human and animal). Many will stretch their normal office schedule to tend an emergency, some will meet you at the office after hours, and a few even make house calls.

And don't forget that vets operate under one huge disadvantage: they can't ask their patients where it hurts.

So, the best time to find a good vet is *before* you need one, which means doing some homework before you get your dog. What factors should you consider when choosing a vet?

- **Proximity & Convenience** - When your pup needs care, you don't want distance to keep you from getting to the office. So, as with family doctors, it's probably not a bad idea to find a vet that's not too far from home.

- **Comfort** - And we're not talking about the waiting-room chairs. Again, as with a family doctor, you want a vet who makes you feel comfortable—both in a professional and personal way.

- **Information** - A good vet is willing to answer your questions, without making you feel dumb or rushed. If you make a call and leave a non-emergency message, it's not unreasonable to expect a call-back the same day.

- **Staff Support** - The receptionists and techs should be friendly and helpful. It's not a bad sign if they seem to be happy where they work. The vet in charge can set the tone for the entire office.

To find out about vets in your area, you can consult the Yellow Pages. You can also check with your state's veterinary medical association. And ask pet-owning neighbors and friends about their vets; if several come highly recommended, they can be at the top of your list. Trainers, groomers and the local animal-control agency may also be of assistance.

Once you've narrowed the list, it's time to make personal inspection visits. However, don't drop in—call for an appointment to meet the doctor and staff, and tour the hospital. According to *Your Dog*, a nifty newsletter published by Tufts University Vet School, here are some things to look for and ask about:

- A facility that looks and smells clean
- A pleasant waiting room that's not too cramped

- Separate dog and cat waiting rooms are a good idea
- Exam rooms, lab space and surgical suites that are clean and orderly
- Separate kennel/cage areas for animal-patients and boarding clients (to keep boarded dogs from being exposed to sick ones)
- Gas-anesthesia equipment in operating rooms
- Emergency and after-hours procedures: do they handle things on-site or refer you to an emergency clinic?

It's a bonus if you find an *American Animal Hospital Association (AAHA)* plaque on the wall. *Your Dog* reports that *AAHA*-accredited hospitals meet rigorous standards for emergency care, surgery and anesthesia, radiology, and nursing care.

As of 1995, only 14 percent of small animal hospitals in the U.S. and Canada were *AAHA* members. So not being an *AAHA* member doesn't mean a hospital won't provide excellent care. But knowing your hospital meets *AAHA* standards may give you additional peace of mind where your pet's health is concerned.

Typical New-Puppy Medical Expenses

Sometimes it seems like young puppies are at the vet every other week. There are the shots and the de-worming, and almost every puppy has some sort of vomiting or digestive upset that scares the heck out of harried and sleep-deprived new pup-parents.

Here's a list of typical expenses, compiled from the medical records of my two current Corgis, Mickey and Callie, covering their first 6 months with us, living near Baltimore, Maryland.

Visit 1 -	Physical	**$30**
	Fecal lab test	**$15**
	K-9 cough vaccine	**$12**
	Sentinel heartworm/flea pills	
	(6-month supply)	**$45**
Visit 2 -	Coronavirus vaccine	**$16**
Visit 3 -	DHLPP combo vaccine	**$16**
Visit 4 -	Coronavirus booster	**$18**
Visit 5 -	DHLPP vaccine	**$18**
	Rabies vaccine	**$18**
	Frontline anti-flea treatment	
	(3 month supply)	**$26**
Visit 6 -	Spaying surgery (female)	**$160**
Visit 7 -	Heartworm test	**$35**
	K-9 cough booster	**$18**
Visit 8 -	Urinary tract infection	
	(unexpected but not uncommon)	
	lab tests, treatment, medication	**$180**
	6-month total	**$603**

Some vets now consider rabies and the DHLPP combo to be "core" required vaccines. Coronavirus, K-9 cough, and Lyme vaccines may be optional, based on your pup's activities, lifestyle, and likelihood of exposure. Be sure to discuss this with your vet to make sure your dog is properly protected.

Prices for veterinary care will obviously vary from place to place and vet to vet—some charge more than others. I share this information just to provide a basic idea of what to expect.

Barring emergency or chronic-care conditions, vet visits and expenses usually decline after the first (and most expensive) 6 months.

Puppy Prep Shopping List: Stuff to Buy

These items are "essentials" (mostly) you'll want to purchase or find *before* you bring your new puppy or dog home. Also included are approximate costs. Prices vary from place to place and store to store. If you have a computer and know how to surf the web, you may get better deals buying from on-line retailers at various pet-supply web sites.

Item		Cost
CRATE	I prefer the plastic travel-style crate. It's lighter, cheaper, easier to move and clean. Gives you the option of buying more than one size to accommodate a growing puppy. Pups often like these better because they're more "den-like" than metal cages. (Don't bother with a bed yet. Pups are more likely to shred 'em than sleep on 'em. See **Crates Are Great** on page 160 for more info.)	**$25 to $100**
LEASH	6-foot, nylon or cotton-web type. Cheaper and more durable than leather. Many puppies chew through at least one leash. If you prefer leather, *wait* until your dog is older and past the leash-chewing stage.	**$5 to $10**
COLLAR	Nylon buckle-type. Your puppy's first collar should be fairly lightweight. And unless your dog is a toy breed, he'll outgrow the first collar.	**$3 to $6**
GROWN-UP COLLARS	The rounded, rolled-style (nylon or leather) is easier on longer coats.	**$5 to $12**
ID TAG	Get one right away. It's a cheap way to make it more likely your dog will be returned if he runs away or gets lost.	**$5**

Item		Cost
FOOD & WATER BOWLS	Stainless steel may be more expensive, but it's chew-proof and easier to clean.	**$5 to $10 each**
BABY GATE(S)	For confining pups to certain areas of your house. More than one may be helpful, depending on your home's floorplan. Essential for housebreaking, & limiting destruction & trouble.	**$30 to $50**
HOUSE-BREAKING AIDES	Potent liquids that smell like dog urine; used outdoors to encourage pups to pee and poop where we want them to.	**$5**
ENZYME CLEANING SOLUTION	Household cleansers don't work on puppy accidents. Cleaners like Simple Solution and Nature's Miracle do, as long as you follow directions.	**$10 to $20 (size varies)**
BITTER APPLE	Yucky-tasting stuff discourages unauthorized chewing. Comes in two types for different situations. **Liquid:** for leashes, rugs, fabric items, and human hands. **Ointment:** for wood cabinets, furniture, and wood trim.	**$10 to $12**
TOYS	Don't be cheap! Quality toys are worth the extra few dollars. Flimsy toys won't last long, and pose a danger to your pup. A variety of chew and play toys will help stave off boredom.	**$3 to $15 each**
TREATS	Get *small* tid-bit types for training rewards. Or simply use pieces of dry kibble-food.	**varies**
BOOKS	Have a few training and dog-health books for reference.	**$20 to $40**
GROOM-ING	Most dogs are bathed too often and combed or brushed too infrequently. Tend your dog's coat with grooming rake, comb and/or brush. Use pump-spray no-rinse shampoos, coat-oil, deodorants.	**varies**

Item		Cost
FLEA & TICK CONTROL	Skip old-style flea/tick collars, sprays and powders. Vets have the newest, most effective treatments. They cost more, but they really work! Current favorites include:	
	Sentinel (monthly combo flea/heartworm pill)	**$50/6 mos.**
	Frontline (topical "spot-on" ointment)	**$30/3 treatments**
FOOD	Dry food is more cost-effective. Look for appropriate nutritional balance, based on puppy's age and activity level. Look for foods made with meat or meat meal, not meat by-products. Avoid foods with chemical preservatives (BHA, BHT and ethoxyquin). Once chosen, stick with one food. Start with small bag until you're sure food agrees with pup's tummy.	**$15 to $25 (20 lb. bag)**

Optional Items Worth Considering:

Item		Cost
EXERCISE PEN	Sold at pet supply stores and through catalogs. May be plastic or metal. Portable pens allow you to set up a "playpen area" indoors or out, of varying size and shape. Great way to give pup a little more freedom, but still keep him safe and confined.	**$50 and up**
LONG LEASH	Same material and construction as standard leash. Many lengths available. 20 or 30-foot is a good choice for extra freedom with security, and for advanced training. (A much better and more cost-effective choice than a retractable leash. Retractables can be clumsy to handle and operate, and the internal mechanism may break and jam.)	**$10 and up (depends on length)**
MICRO-CHIP ID	Scannable electronic ID "tag" injected by vet. Most shelters and animal hospitals have equipment for identifying lost dogs with chips.	**varies**

Head Halters: New Way to Walk Your Dog

How can you teach your dog to walk calmly on a leash without pulling? It's not easy. Some people use "choke" chain/training collars, which can work well if *used properly*—or may *hurt* your dog if used incorrectly.

Some people try harnesses. These may actually make the problem worse, since the structure of a harness actually encourages pulling. Only dogs with delicate necks, soft windpipes, or flat faces that inhibit breathing should use harnesses.

In recent years, a new alternative has become popular: the *Head Halter*. There are several brands available, but they're similar in design and all offer a gentle yet effective means of controlling your dog.

Regular collars are attached to your dog's neck—and dog necks (other than in toy breeds) are fairly muscular and strong. Head halters fit over a dog's face (see picture)—and the face is much more sensitive.

Head halters can be especially helpful with large-breed puppies. Labs, Goldens, and Rottweilers (and mixes of these breeds) are very popular these days. Hardly a week goes by that I don't see a client who has underestimated how quickly these pups get big and strong. Pulling on-leash may not seem that important when your brand-new pup is 15 or 20 pounds.

But a 20-pound cutie-pie becomes a 50-pound monster before you know it. And it's much easier to deal with teaching your dog to walk properly on-leash when he's small. So, whatever collar option you choose, get to work on this sooner rather than later.

A head halter lets you to lead your dog with minimal force. However, dogs naturally resist anything that goes around the muzzle. The first few times a halter is put on, most dogs try to push it off with their paws or shake it off. Getting accustomed to it takes practice for both you and your dog.

It's a big mistake to throw the head halter on your dog and rush out for a walk. Try this instead:

STEP 1	Have small tasty treats ready. Slip the nose loop over your dog's muzzle—and distract him with a couple of treats. Try to clip the neck piece behind his head—and give him another couple of treats. (This is easier with a helper—one person handles the dog, the other supplies the treats.) Leave the halter on for just a few seconds. Then take it off and give your dog another treat. Do this a few times a day, for a few days. Most dogs start to accept the new feeling of a loose loop around their muzzles once they realize they can still open their mouths without restriction. Leave the halter on for a few seconds longer each time. Keep those treats coming! You want your dog to have a positive association with the halter.
STEP 2	If this seems to be working, then clip the leash to the ring under your dog's chin. *Gently* encourage him to follow you. Use treats. *Don't force him.* Let him get the feel of walking with this thing on his face. Practice this indoors a few times a day for several more days.
STEP 3	Next, try taking him outside—preferably in a yard or some-place where your dog feels safe. He's still getting used to the halter. Practice "gentle leading." You don't have to pull hard to get your dog to follow.
STEP 4	When you feel ready, start walking your dog on his normal route with the head halter. Make sure he's still got his regular collar on, in case you need to switch from the head halter if he resists.
PROPER FIT	The neck strap should be fairly snug. The nose loop should allow your dog to open his mouth normally.
PROPER USE	Don't give your dog more than a few inches of slack in the leash. *Don't jerk the leash.* Use gentle smooth motions. As *soon* as your dog does what you want (walking or sitting calmly, not pulling or jumping) *relax all leash tension.* To reduce forward pulling or jumping, *gently* turn your dog's head slightly sideways toward you. To get your dog to sit, gently pull the leash forward and upward. Do the same thing if he tries to jump to greet someone. *Always praise and relax leash-tension* when he does what you want.

.Until your dog gets comfortable with the feel of the head-halter, bring lots of tidbit-treats with you on walks. Once you start using it, don't stop! Eventually, most dogs associate the head-halter with walks, and will eagerly put it on.

Don't get discouraged! It may take a little time, but most dogs adjust well to the head halters. Used properly, they can end pulling altogether—and make walks with your pal fun instead of an ordeal!

It's important to get the halter that fits your dog's *current* size. Yes, your Beagle-size Labrador pup will outgrow this first halter, but until he does, you'll have the right size for starting the teaching process. If you think a head halter may be the right choice for your dog, but you're still uncertain about how to use one, consult a trainer. The two brands most readily available are:

GENTLE LEADER	May be a little more expensive, but also more adjustable. Still important to get the proper size. Appears more sturdy. 5 sizes. Comes with a superb instruction booklet. Instructional video available.
HALTI	May be less expensive, and a bit easier to locate. Less adjustable, but comes in 6 sizes. Lighter material. Skimpy instructions.

Training with "The Two Commandments"

Why only *two* commandments? Because dog training is (fortunately) simpler than religion: we don't need another eight. You may already have seen these and other guidelines elsewhere in this book. But these are the "biggies," so I thought it was worth featuring them on their very own page. With time and practice, you'll find them helpful in preventing (or solving) most typical puppy behavior problems.

1st Commandment of Dog Training:

If there are things you *don't* want your dog to do, *don't* let him do them!

This is how you keep such doggie favorites as jumping, nipping, chewing your stuff, and food-snatching from becoming lifelong habits. But it's not enough to say "No"...

2nd Commandment:

If there are things you *do* want your dog to do, *teach* him—the sooner the better!

For example: most puppies jump to greet visitors. If you only stop your pup from jumping, and that's the only way he knows to get attention, he'll try it again. But if you teach him an alternative—like "Sit-stay"—and reward him when he does it, he'll learn to do that instead. It really works!

Law #1:

When puppies do something wrong, there's a human co-conspirator.

When a puppy grabs an unguarded sandwich off the coffee table, well...a human left it there, right? We can't blame a puppy for thinking, "Oooo, that must be for me!"

Law #2:

Learn from each mistake how to keep it from happening again.

For example, if you control the sandwich (taking it with you when you get up for a drink) or control the dog (taking *him* along when you leave the sandwich), your pup doesn't get a chance to help himself to your lunch. Simple!

A Dog's Bill of Rights

If your dog could talk, this is what he'd say to you:

I'm a dog. Since you've added me to your family, you have the right to expect that I will grow up and be a good pet and companion. But dogs can't do that without your help—and without your understanding that dogs also have the following rights:

* To have our people promise to assure our health & safety at all times. We trust you and rely on you for proper medical care when we need it, and high-quality food for our daily diet.

* To be part of your family—not to be tied up in the yard. Or kept in the garage. Or shut away in the basement.

* To be trained to have good manners. We're capable of learning anything you want us to learn—but we need you to teach us how to behave in the company of people.

* To be properly restrained by a leash when we're outdoors, so we can't run off and be hurt or killed.

- To humane use of a crate (our very own safe "den") and baby gates to keep us from roaming your house and getting into trouble when we're young. If we go to the bathroom in the house, or chew things we're not supposed to chew, it's because we either didn't know better, or we couldn't help it. TEACH US!

- To never be hit, kicked, screamed at or otherwise physically or emotionally abused. Please remember that we have feelings, just like people.

- To be spayed or neutered while we're young, so we can't accidentally add to the population of unwanted puppies. We don't have to breed to be happy.

- To be included in family activities whenever possible. We're "pack" animals, so nothing makes us happier than to be with our human pack. If you teach us good manners, we'll be welcome wherever we go.

- To be treated with kindness, patience and love — the way you'd like to be treated.

Thank You!

Crates Are Great!

Call it a crate or a kennel. But crate-training is the single easiest way to housebreak your puppy and keep him out of trouble. Used properly, a crate is not a prison. If you start right away—and the *right way*—most puppies can quickly learn to like their crates. With a little effort, you can teach your puppy to regard his crate as "home."

Why does crate training work?

Good question. Simple answer: by instinct, dogs are den animals. Wild canines tend to use very small, snug burrows for the birth and raising of their babies. So dog-brains are wired to be comfortable in small, dark, enclosed spaces. My own Welsh Corgis love to squeeze under couches and beds. They barely fit—but that's where they go when they want some quiet time to themselves.

Mickey is living proof that it's not hard to get pups to love their crates

From the time they're very young, pups prefer not to soil the area where they eat and sleep. So using a properly-sized crate encourages puppies to become housebroken quickly and easily.

What size should a crate be?

When it comes to crates, *size does matter!* Common mistake: buying a crate that's too big. *People* generally prefer big, open and airy. *Dogs* prefer small, dark and cozy. A crate only needs to be big enough for your pup to walk in without crouching or ducking his head; to turn around in (and pups can turn in a very small area); and to lie down. Given more space, many dogs will sleep stretched out. With less space, they'll sleep comfortably curled up in a little ball.

A correct-size crate helps in potty-training, by giving a pup motivation to avoid going to the bathroom where he sleeps (and eats—more on that later). If a crate is too big, a puppy won't think twice about eliminating at one end and curling up at the other.

Also, if a puppy has lots of room to move around, this extra motion is going to speed up his digestive system, and he'll need to go to the bathroom at shorter intervals.

Many folks with large-breed puppies get a crate big enough to accommodate the grown-up version of their baby. But that means the crate may be too big for the not-yet-housebroken new arrival. There are two solutions to this problem:

- buy a smaller "starter" crate to use during the crucial early months when potty training is paramount;
- figure out how to make the huge crate smaller, possibly by using a large plastic storage bin (bottom out) to fill the rear of the crate and create a wall, thus trimming the size of the space to be filled by your puppy. Some crates come with an adjustable partition.

Should we get a metal crate or a plastic one?

If people ask before they buy a crate, I suggest getting the molded-plastic, travel-style item rather than the metal cage-type, for several reasons. Plastic crates comes in a larger variety of sizes. They're much less expensive (so buying two to accommodate your growing pup isn't an economic hardship).

They're easier to take apart and clean. They're much lighter, so they're easier to move around the house, as needed. They fit more easily into cars and other vehicles, enabling you to keep your dog safe when traveling. And they're much more denlike—smaller, darker, cozier—factors which make puppies more comfortable when inside.

But if you already have a metal crate, do what you can to make sure it's the proper size for your puppy. To make it more cozy, you can drape an old blanket or large towel over the top and sides, leaving some open space near the floor to allow for air circulation.

What should I use a crate for?

This is where your puppy will sleep, nap, chew and eat. Used properly, a crate is a combination crib and playpen—items without which parents would never survive the infancy and toddler-hood of their human kids!

The crate is where your puppy can feel safe and secure—and where you know he can't get into trouble during those times when you can't supervise him.

Feed your pup his meals in his crate. Since most dogs love eating, this will help your pup build a positive association with his crate from the day you bring him home. Just slide the dish to the rear of the crate, so your pup has to go in to chow down. You don't have to close the door. Don't leave uneaten food. Remove the dish after a maximum of 20 minutes. If he doesn't eat it all, he'll be hungry for the next meal.

How can I not feel guilty about putting my puppy in a crate?

By remembering that puppies don't mind being in crates, as long as you make sure they have ample opportunity to get out, go to the bathroom, and get needed exercise through walks and playtime with you. When it's time to put your pup in his "den," give him lots of praise and a little tidbit-treat. If you have a positive attitude toward the crate, so will your dog.

How long can I keep my puppy in a crate?

For young pups, about one hour per month of age, plus up to an hour. So a 3-month old puppy should be able to go up to 4 hours in a crate—assuming, of course, that he's had a chance to go potty before you put him in, and that there's no water or food in the crate with him. Obviously, if he's eating and drinking while in his crate, what goes in must come out.

How long should we use a crate?

Dogs are puppies until around 2 years of age. For the first year of your pup's life, it's probably safer to crate him whenever you have to leave him home alone. Even after he's housebroken, he may be prone to destructive chewing of all sorts of household items—including the living room sofa!

This sort of thing lands many young dogs in animal shelters—but it's not the dogs' fault. It's ours, for giving them the chance to get into trouble. Crating a pup eliminates the possibility of major misbehavior.

My two Corgis are no longer puppies, but they still eat in their crates (with the doors open). This makes it less likely one will try to munch on the other's food. They also travel safely inside their crates. And when we visit friends or relatives, we may use the crates for short periods of time when we can't watch our dogs, to keep them from tasting "forbidden fruit" in an unfamiliar environment.

How can I teach my dog to enter his crate on command?

This can be both easy and fun. First, decide what everyone in your household will call the crate. We decided "room" was friendlier than "crate." Then, just before mealtime, take 10 pieces of your pup's dry kibble. Place one nugget 2 inches inside the crate, so all he has to do to get it is stick his head in. Encourage your puppy to go get the treat by saying: "Go into your room!" If he does, reward him with lots of praise.

Repeat the game, but put the next piece a little further inside. Each time your pup gets the treat, praise him. Your goal is to get to the point where you can toss a food-nugget all the way to the back of the crate, and your pup will dive in after it, on the command "Go into your room!"

Some pups hesitate. If yours isn't eager to follow the food, gently pick him up and place him in the crate, making sure to repeat the command phrase, along with generous praise. But don't force him in if he kicks and screams. Just keep playing this game, possibly using food morsels more mouth-watering (tiny pieces of a hot dog or American cheese might do the trick).

Playing this game when your pup is hungry increases the chance of success.

Repeat this game 2 or more times a day for a week or so. Chances are, you'll have your pup going after those food nuggets in a few days. Once you do, you're going to *change the rules*.

Instead of using the food as a *lure* to get him to go into his crate, you're going to start asking him to go in first—then giving him the treat as a *reward*. The first few times, your pup may balk. He's thinking: "Hey, that's not how the game goes!" If he does, you'll gently pick him up, place him inside while saying the command phrase, then immediately give him the reward and praise—even though the only reason he went in was because you put him in. In a short time, most pups understand and happily play by the new rules. After a while, you can make the treat-rewards random and occasional—and soon eliminate them altogether.

In a few short days, you'll be able to amaze your friends and relatives by showing them how your pup goes into his "room" just because you ask him to. Don't forget to say thank you and give him lots of praise when he does.

What about special treats?

Another great way to get your pup to love his crate: once or twice a day, give him a special treat or food-bearing toy that he only gets in his crate. It could be a favorite chew toy. Or a rubber *Kong* toy or hollow sterilized "marrow" bone with some peanut butter stuffed in it. Or a peeled, ready-to-eat baby carrot. Best if it's something that keeps him busy for a while.

Should I put a bed or blanket in his crate?

Probably not, because what puppies usually do with bedding is chew it up, pee on it, or both. Peeing on bedding allows a pup to push it off to the side and ignore it. And it may be days before you know that your puppy is doing this. Puppies are usually perfectly comfortable lying on the cool crate floor. Certainly don't buy an expensive bed for a puppy. If you want to put something soft in, a piece of an old blanket or towel will do.

Should I put toys in with him?

Yes! A couple of safe and sturdy chew toys will help keep him busy and happy. Don't put plush toys in the crate; sharp teeth can easily shred these, enabling a pup to swallow and possibly choke on stuffing and squeakers.

What about his water dish?

In general, don't leave water in the crate. If your pup drinks, he's going to have to pee in there. Also, puppies tend to play in and tip over water dishes, leaving a wet crate and soaked dog. If your pup is going to be crated for four hours or more, look in the bird department of the pet store for something called a "Coop Cup." This is a metal bracket that attaches to the crate door; the bracket holds a small stainless-steel bowl up off the crate floor. You can put one or two ice cubes in the bowl. As the ice melts slowly, your pup can sip a little water if he needs to, without drinking enough to force him to urinate in his crate.

What if I can't make it home in time to walk my crated puppy on a fair & reasonable schedule?

Then you need to make alternate arrangements. Maybe there's a neighbor (adult or responsible older child) you'd trust with a house key and the job of walking your pup on schedule. Offer to pay something. Most areas are also served by professional dog-walking services. If you need such a service, check with your vet's office for recommendations, or check the Yellow Pages.

What if my puppy cries at night when he's put in his crate?

It's natural for a new pup to feel lonely the first few nights he's away from his mom and siblings. You can help him get over this by *not* doing what many people do: putting the pup and crate in the basement or garage or kitchen, far away from any other living thing.

Instead, for at least the first few nights, put the crate within arm's reach of your bed. Play with your pup before bedtime to tire him out, walk him so he can go potty, then put him in the crate when you're ready for bed yourself. If he fusses, *don't* sweet-talk him with a soothing voice. Pups interpret that as praise for crying. But don't *yell* at him—remember, he's just a lonely baby.

The instant he starts crying, reach over, tap the side or top of the crate, and say "*No—Shhh—Quiet*" in a neutral voice. Then, if he's quiet for even a second or two, quietly praise him and tell him "*Bedtime—quiet. Good puppy.*" Repeat this as often as you need to, until he falls asleep.

During the night, he can hear you and smell you. He'll know you're close by. And he'll be less lonely.

Keep in mind that puppies less than 4 months old may not be able to sleep through the night without needing to go potty. If your pup fusses in the middle of the night, get up, put his leash on and take him outside. Encourage him to go the bathroom. If he does, praise him quietly—and put him right back to bed in his crate. Don't stop to play with him. On the other hand, if you take him out and he doesn't go (after giving him a few minutes in his special "potty area"), he goes right back to bed.

Yes, having him sleeping near your bed means you'll hear every sound he makes. But that's the idea. If he needs to go to the bathroom, and he's at the other end of the house, you're going to wake up to a messy crate and messy pup. Personally, I'd much rather get up for five minutes in the middle of the night than spend an hour the next morning cleaning both crate and dog.

Most puppies can quickly learn to go to bed in their crates quietly. And as they get older, they'll be able to sleep through the night. As time passes, you can decide if you want your dog to continue to sleep in your bedroom, or move the crate elsewhere.

EXTRA TIPS:

Never use a crate as punishment

If your pup's been naughty and you need a break—and he needs a "time-out"—make sure you're both calm when you crate him. Give him praise and maybe even a tidbit-treat when you shut that door.

Start short

When you bring your pup home, get him accustomed to crating by putting him in for short periods of time while you're still home to correct him if he cries, and to praise him when he's quiet. Getting him used to the crate while you're home will keep him from associating the crate with being left home alone.

Only quiet dogs come out

Try to avoid letting your pup out of his crate when he's crying. If you do, you'll be teaching him he can get what he wants simply by making a fuss. An *exception* to this is if you think he's got to go potty—*NOW*! If that's the case, then be ready to get his leash on and whisk him outside to his potty area. If he indeed relieves himself, great! Praise him—and then put him right back into the crate if that's where you need him to be at that moment.

Collar safety

Make sure your pup's collar fits well (no more than 2-3 fingers should fit under it). Make sure there's nothing in the crate for him to catch his collar on. If there is, remove the collar when he's crated.Don't force the issue

Don't force the issue

Some pups may have had negative experiences with crates before they come to live with us. If your pup freaks out at the sight of a crate, don't force him into it. Consult a trainer.

Potty Training

Potty training, house-breaking, house-training… by any name, it's the art of *minimizing* your puppy's chances to have indoor bathroom accidents—and *maximizing* her chance to go potty outdoors. In the process, you'll be teaching her that *outside* is the accepted place to relieve herself.

Sounds simple. But the failure to master this challenge may be the leading reason we end up wondering: *Why on Earth did we get a puppy in the first place?* But the process doesn't have to be torture—unless we humans cheat and try to take short-cuts. Then it'll seem like *endless* torture.

I recently got a call from former clients, a nice family with a 2-year-old Bichon. I hadn't seen them since their cute, smart dog was about 6 months old. And they're calling me because—*for months now*—he's been peeing and pooping in the house. Which means this pooch never actually got his potty-training degree.

Despite advice to the contrary, these folks allowed their not-quite-house-trained pup to have unsupervised freedom all over their house. They left food out so he could nibble whenever he felt like it. They allowed *him* to decide whether or not he felt like going for a potty walk in rainy weather. In short, they followed a sure-fire path to disaster.

I reminded them of all the basics to which they must return—immediately and without fail. I'm hopeful they'll be successful. But I also warned them that failure to do what *must* be done—even if it's inconvenient—means this problem will *not* go away.

Let's start with some facts:

- Young puppies simply don't have the physical ability to control when and where they go to the bathroom—any more than a baby in diapers does. When they gotta go, they go. And different puppies potty-train at different rates. So don't compare your pup to others.

- Things that make puppies need to pee or poop: sleeping, eating, drinking, playing and moving around. If it sounds like everything makes them need to go—you're right!

- A crated puppy should be able to go 1 hour per month of age plus up to one additional hour without having to go potty (example: a 3-month-old can go up to 4 hours). For uncrated puppies, all bets are off. (See **Crates Are Great!** on page 160.)

Make sure you've got a proper-size crate in which your pup will sleep overnight, eat her meals 2 or 3 times a day, and rest or chew—safe and out of trouble—whenever she can't be supervised by an adult.

You have two goals:
- ❧ teaching the concept - this comes first
- ❧ eliminating accidents - this happens when you become more proficient and your pup gets older

Here's a typical schedule for a 3-month-old pup that'll help you potty-train her as painlessly as possible:

6 to 7 a.m.

Puppy wakes up. Out for a walk. Give pup food and water. Walk again. 15 minutes of fun with you (combo of play & training). Out for another walk. Back into the crate.

8 a.m.

One more walk before you leave for work.

Noon

You or someone else (neighbor, pal, professional dog-walker) has to give puppy a mid-day walk and short exercise break. Feed mid-day meal (up to 6 months) and water. Walk again. Back in the crate.

4 p.m.

Walk. Water. Play 10-15 minutes. Walk. Back in crate.

5 to 6 p.m.

Home from work! Walk. Water. Feed dinner. Walk. Back in crate. Eat your dinner!

7 p.m.

Walk. Play & training for 20-30 minutes. Walk.

Evening

> Supervised limited freedom and playtime. Walk every 1-2 hours, or when your pup looks like he's thinking about going (more frequently if pup is very active).

8 p.m.

> Pick up water (2-3 hours before bedtime).

10 to 11 p.m.

> Bedtime. Last walk. Pup in crate. Sweet dreams!

If you stay up later, take your puppy on a potty-walk as the last thing before lights-out. This may buy you an extra 15-30 minutes of sleep in the morning. Or it may not—some young pups wake with the sun.

Younger pups need to go out more often, older pups less. But remember your part of the bargain: you must take your pup out on a fair schedule. Asking a puppy to go 7 hours in a crate is not fair. Allowing your pup to sneak off to pee on the rug in the next room and then punishing him isn't fair. Rolling over and trying to ignore your pup's crying at sunrise is not fair. Your puppy is relying on you to do what needs to be done.

A young puppy in a comfortable room-temperature home doesn't need constant access to water. But when he does drink, let him have all he wants.

The schedule is a guideline, not gospel. If you think your pup may need to go, then don't go by the clock: just take him out. If he goes, that's great (and most pups will at least pee a few drops no matter how recently they just went). You get an emptied puppy, and he gets praise. If he doesn't go, no big deal.

With younger pups, a good policy is— when in doubt, take 'em out.

I'd rather take a puppy out 4 or 5 extra times and find out he didn't have to go than to guess the opposite, not take him out and find out I was wrong. Picture this as a board-game called *Potty-Training*: every time he successfully goes to the bathroom outside, you take one step forward. He gets praise, and you get closer to your goal.

Every time you guess wrong and don't take him out, and he has an indoor accident, you lose *three* steps: 1) you feel like an idiot; 2) you have to clean up the mess; and 3) you blew an opportunity to teach him what you want him to do.

The truth is, when our puppies have indoor accidents, it's most likely our fault. It usually means we weren't paying attention. Here are a few house-training tips:

- Use a crate, exercise pen and/or baby gates to limit your pup's freedom in the house.
- Never let a loose, untrained pup out of your sight.
- Establish a schedule—for eating, walks and bedtime. Stick to it—*every* day. Puppies don't know it's Sunday.
- Find a high-quality food that agrees with your pup's tummy—and stick to it. Every time you change foods, you risk a bout of diarrhea.
- If you catch your pup in mid-accident, a loud "No!" or hand-clap may startle him into stopping. Scoop him up and outside immediately, and let him finish. (You may need to give him a few minutes to calm down.) Even if he's got nothing left, praise him outside anyway.
- If you find an accident and don't know how long it's been there, clean it up and forget about it. If you scold your pup more than a few seconds to a minute after he's done the deed, he'll have no idea what he did wrong.

If your pup *did* have an accident more than a minute ago, more than a minute ago, and you didn't know it, then *you weren't doing your job.* Don't blame your puppy—learn from your mistakes — and you and your pup will do better next time.

- *Never* hit your pup with a rolled-up newspaper, or rub his nose in an accident. These methods not only don't accomplish anything—they're cruel.
- Avoid getting impatient with your pup when he seems slow to go outdoors. Encourage him gently and cheerfully.
- If you scold him for being slow, he may get more and more nervous—and *only* go when you're not watching, which means someplace *indoors* where he can hide from you for a few seconds—such as behind the sofa.

Captain's Potty-Log, Stardate 2001.0

One other thing you might want to try. With Mickey and Callie, we had the complicated situation of two puppies—and two people who walked the dogs at different times of the day. There were times when the other partner wasn't there to supply crucial information about what our pups did *earlier*, and what they need to do *now*.

So we started a data-base of sorts. We put a pad and pen on the kitchen counter—a potty log-book. Whoever took the pups out wrote down the time and what each dog did. This accomplished several things:

- It allowed us to see developing patterns—dogs tend to be fairly regular about their bathroom habits. We saw how the pattern changed as they got older. For instance, a pup may poop 4 times a day when younger, then only 3 times when older.

- Major advantage: the person in charge of the bedtime walk can see at a glance if the day's poop-production quota has been met. If it has, then the final walk can be a quick one.

- On the other hand, if your pup is one poop short—and you don't want to be awakened by a crying dog at 4 in the morning—you know you have to give your puppy ample opportunity to take care of business.

- Even if you only have one pup, the potty-log can still be helpful in house-training.

Your puppy may not become house-trained in 2 weeks like Annie did. (That had more to do with her than me.) But if you follow these guidelines, it will happen. Good luck!

Clean-Up Tip

For clean-up of accidents, household cleansers don't do the job. Best bet: one of several *enzyme solutions* sold at pet-supply stores. Make sure you follow directions on the package.

Puppy School 202

The Purpose of Training

Now we'll cover some easy and enjoyable training lessons for you and your puppy to work on together. You won't achieve overnight perfection. But these fundamental behavioral building blocks not only start your pup on the road to good manners; they can also help you solve common behavior problems as your puppy grows up.

Why is puppy education so important? Because teaching "*Sit*" is more than getting his rump on the floor. When you teach your dog to understand commands, you're creating a common vocabulary that helps you and your dog communicate. If your puppy learns that sitting and looking cute is the way to get you to play with him, he'll do *that* instead of jumping on you or biting your socks.

Real-life example: When my Mickey was a puppy, she'd happily hurl herself at us to get our attention. As cute as she was, this behavior was, frankly, a real pain the neck. Then my wife Susan noticed that every now and then, Mick would sit and tap us gently with her paw. So Susan called that action "*Please*" and taught Mickey to use that gesture instead of jumping on us. Mickey learned that her adorable little "*Please*" tap was the way to get what she wanted—and she gave up jumping on us.

"Perfection" means your pup does everything you ask eagerly and instantly, the *first time* you ask. Should you shoot for perfection? Sure! Why not? But few dogs are perfect (few people, too, I might add). How well your puppy learns this stuff is a product of his intelligence and personality—as well as your ability as a teacher, and how much time and effort you devote to training.

So a more realistic goal should be "near-perfection": your pup does what you ask on the first or second time she hears the command, with little or no hesitation—and better than 90 percent of the time. And almost every pup and human should be able to attain this level of success—*eventually*.

It's not going to happen the first weeks (or even months) you and your dog work together. But if you work consistently with your pup, by the end of her first year, there should be days when she really listens and does what you ask with a level of accomplishment you wouldn't have dreamed possible during those first uncertain weeks of canine education.

However, at this age, there will be days when your pup might as well be from Mars, for all the English she seems to understand. Does this mean you and she are failures? Absolutely not! It just means your job as pup-professor is not quite complete.

Keep working during your puppy's second year. Try to add some new and challenging tasks. Tricks and agility training are fun for people and dogs alike. You can get some ideas about advanced subjects from the various books and web sites mentioned at the end of this book.

Whatever happens, *please* don't give up! I don't want you and your puppy to end up adding to the statistics of failure. I want you to have the kind of wonderful life with your dog that I had with Annie, and continue to have with Mickey and Callie. If you stick with the program, *you can do it!*

Remember, you're not being graded on this dog-training thing. Having and training a dog is supposed to be a fun part of life. And life, as they say, is an open-book test. If you're having a problem, and don't know how to solve it, there's somebody out there who can help you. Read a book. Try a video. Ask your vet. Call a trainer. The answers are available, and not all that hard to find.

If you put in the effort to do this right, there's a very good chance you'll be rewarded far beyond your dreams.

Okay? Let's get to work.

When I teach group pup classes...

- ❧ We meet one hour a week, for seven weeks. In following this puppy-school curriculum at home, you can break each class program into "bite-size" chunks, so to speak.

- ❧ This gives you more flexibility—and it's actually preferable to do **two or three ten-minute mini-classes each day** instead of working for an entire hour. **Puppies have short attention-spans and do better in mini-sessions.**

- ❧ Just be sure to keep practicing each command until your puppy does it well. And be sure to **add new things** to learn as you go along. This will help keep your puppy (and you!) from growing bored.

To Treat, or Not to Treat

There's a great debate raging between trainers who still favor the old-fashioned ways and those who embrace the newer, increasingly popular *positive-reinforcement* methods of pup education. Among their disagreements: whether or not to use treat-rewards during training.

Old-style trainers believe that dogs should always be expected to respond to commands, without resorting to treats. And those trainers are right—*up to a point*. It's true that you won't always have treats handy—but you always have a pocketful of praise. So *praise*, these trainers say, should be the currency with which you reward your dog.

Advocates of more modern training methods believe in generous and frequent use of treats. Why? Because behavioral scientists know that food rewards help dogs focus on and remember new lessons.

So I suggest using treats as a bonus, beyond the praise you *always* want to give *instantly* when your puppy does something right. Here's how I think they work best:

- When teaching something new, use treats on many of the first few repetitions.

- When your pup seems to understand the command, start giving the treats intermittently—at random.

- As training progresses, trim treat-rewards to one or two early in a training session—and then skip the treats until the end of the session. Giving a treat as a final bonus helps your dog remember training as a fun activity.

- Be careful not to overdo treat-rewards. It's possible to create a situation where your dog will only do what you ask when he knows in advance there's a treat waiting for him.

- Giving treats at random taps into your dog's natural optimism: if he *ever* got a treat for sitting, for instance, he'll *always* remember that a wondrous thing happened. And he'll believe that he can make it happen *again*, even if it doesn't happen every time.

"Phantom" Treats

❧ Use your dog's natural optimism to help avoid over-use of treats. Sometimes, after giving a food reward, you can *pretend* to have a treat by holding your finger-tips the same way, and moving your hand as if there's a treat there.

❧ To a dog's nose, your hand still *smells* like the last treat. When your dog does what you ask, instead of getting the *real* treat, she gets to lick your fingers while you reward her with verbal praise and "skritches."

- Why deprive yourself of an excellent teaching tool?
- Best treats: small tidbits. Many dogs respond well to pieces of their dry kibble. Others only perk up for something special—you can try small flavored treats, bits of cheese, or chunks of chicken hot-dogs.

Puppy School - Class 1

Introduction & Tips to Use Now!

First Commandment of Dog Training:

If there are things you **don't** want your pup to do, then **don't** let him do them! (This book will help you accomplish that.)

Second Commandment:

If there are things you **do** want your pup to do, **teach** him—the sooner the better!

- Dogs like to feel good. They like praise and "sweet-talk." They don't like to be scolded. Show them what you *want* them to do, and you can teach them what not to do.

- Dogs can learn to understand a hundred or more words and expressions, so *talk* to them often. They also "read" human tone of voice and body language.

- So don't yell at your dog. Teach yourself to be *firm yet gentle.*

- Training should never be a chore—for you or your pup. Be upbeat and happy when you train. Remember: your pup is trying his best to learn what you want him to know. So be *patient & positive.* If you make training fun, your pup will love to learn!

- When using a leash and collar, be gentle. It only takes a slight tug to make your point. Some behaviorists believe a tug on the collar reminds a puppy of when Mama would correct him by grabbing him by the scruff of the neck and shaking him gently. Leash and collar corrections allow us to do the same thing in a safe way. Do *not* pick your pup up by the scruff of his neck.

If your pup does something wrong...

- ❧ **Correct** him—don't **punish** him. Punishment doesn't teach him anything.
- ❧ **Correction** teaches him what you want him to do.

- Avoid giving commands you can't enforce. When your pup gets a chance to *ignore* your command, he learns it's OK to not listen. It's *not* OK!! OK?

- So teach yourself to hold off on a command until you have *physical control* of your pup: hand on collar or hand on leash.

- The foundation of all training is the ability to get your pup to pay attention to you.

- Pups have to earn freedom.

- Never give an untrained pup free run of your home: that's asking for trouble. Use baby gates and doors to keep your pup in the room with you—use his leash to keep him from getting in trouble.

- If you're not there to supervise your pup's behavior, it's OK to confine him in a small, safe, uncarpeted space (like your kitchen). Or to put him inside his exercise pen. It's also OK to tell him it's "Naptime" and put him in his crate with a favorite chew toy.

To get your pup to *love* his crate—*never* crate your dog in anger. It's his "den," not a prison cell. *Always* tell him he's good when he goes in. Give him reward-treats at random intervals. Feed his meals in his crate. (See **Crates Are Great!** on page 160 for more crate tips.)

- *Always* pick up after your dog when he poops outside. Simplest method: slip a plastic bag over your hand like a glove; pick up the poop; turn the bag inside out; tie off the top; deposit in the dumpster or trash. Some people use grocery or newspaper bags, but I'm always afraid those bags may have a strategic hole in them. So I prefer "virgin" 1-gallon-size bags available at any grocery store. I never leave the house without 3 or 4 in my pocket.

- Unscooped poop is an eyesore (and not too nice to the nose, either). It's also a *health hazard*—to your pup, you and your kids.

To reiterate the math: if 10 dogs on your block each poop in the same area twice a day, they'll produce 20 piles a day, 140 piles a week, and *7300 PILES A YEAR!* Sooner or later, you and/or your dog will step in one. Cleaning poop out from between your pup's toes (and the convolutions on the bottom of your athletic shoes) is *really fun!*

Puppy School - Class 2

Basics & Reminders

- *Be patient & positive!* Use 1-or-2-word commands.
- Until your pup learns to respond both reliably *and* well, *don't* give a command you can't *enforce.* That will only teach him he doesn't have to listen to you. *He does!*
- If you use *treat-rewards,* don't give a treat every time your pup does something right. Use treats sparingly.
- When teaching a new command, say it *once* as you show your pup what you want him to do.
- *Praise* him every time he does what you ask, whether it was his idea or yours. *Repeat* until he starts to do it on his own. Once he seems to understand the command, then say it once and give him a chance to do it on his own. If he doesn't, *repeat* the command word at the same time as you gently-but-firmly show him what to do.
- Repeat this process until he starts responding readily.
- It's fine to use *praise* without *treats.* Even if you use occasional treats, *always* use praise!
- Pay attention to your *tone of voice.* Sound *cheerful* but *firm.* Remember, you're giving commands, not making requests.

Biting, Nipping, Mouthing & Growling

Not allowed. Stop these before they become bad habits. Try any and all of the following "anti-bite" strategies:

- If your pup nips you, do collar or leash correction, with a firm *"No."* Give him a toy instead. *Praise* when he chews the toy.
- **OR**— yelp loudly. (You won't have to pretend—sharp puppy teeth hurt!) This mimics the reaction of another puppy who's been bitten too hard, and helps your puppy learn to avoid this behavior. Offer toy instead.
- **OR**—spray hand with *Bitter Apple* (nasty-tasting but harmless liquid sold at most pet-supply stores). Give him a taste of your hand. If he turns away, offer a chew toy and praise.
- **OR**—remove your hand. Say *"No."* Offer toy instead. Praise when he chews the toy.
- **OR**—put your hand *further* into his mouth. This is unpleasant to many pups and helps convince them to stop.

- **OR**—Grab pup's body in a gentle hug. *Gently* hold his muzzle as you say *"No."* Do not use enough pressure to hurt him. *Hold* until he stops struggling. A this point, many pups will start licking instead of nipping. Maintain the body-hug as you release his muzzle and see what he does. Praise kisses—but repeat the muzzle-hold if he nips again. Be prepared to repeat this until your pup licks instead of nipping. **DON'T use this method on a large, strong, or aggressive puppy.**

"Watch Me"

WHY   Before your pup can learn commands, he has to learn to pay attention to you—to make eye contact when you want him to.

HOW   Try the following methods —

1- Treat Method

- Hold treat in front of pup's nose
- Say *"Watch Me"*
- Slowly move treat to your eye level
- Make eye contact - give praise & treat
- Phase out treat-use by *pretending* you have one and moving the "phantom treat" toward your eyes

---

2- Voice Only

- Say your pup's name and *"Watch Me"* in a happy voice
- Praise even the slightest eye contact

3- Chin Lift

- Say *"Watch Me"*
- Use fingers to gently lift his chin
- Make eye contact - give praise

"Sit"

WHY   Provides means of controlling pup's behavior. For instance, a sitting puppy isn't jumping, chewing or running away. Building block for *"Sit-Stay."*

HOW   Two equally good ways —

1- "Rump-Scoop" Method

- Put one hand on pup's collar under his chin; other hand on his rump, just above his tail
- *Don't* push down on hips; pups naturally resist this
- As you say '*Sit,*" scoop pup into sitting position by *gently* pushing up and back on his chest as you tuck his rump under him
- *Praise* (with or without treat)

2- Treat Method

- Hold pup on a short leash (to keep him from grabbing for the treat)
- Get pup's attention
- As you say *"Sit,"* move treat up over pup's head & slightly back
- If he doesn't sit on his own, use free hand to *gently* scoop pup's rear down (same as first method above)
- When he sits, give treat reward—and *praise!*
- Phase out the treats, but keep using verbal command and hand movement
- Eventually hand movement becomes optional

Puppy School - Class 3

"Come"

WHY   Puppies do not naturally come when called. They'd rather play *"Chase Me"*—and you usually can't catch a pup who doesn't want to be caught. So teach the *"Come"* command early and carefully.

HOW   Until your pup learns to respond reliably, *don't* give this command unless he's on a leash. Hold the leash and take 2 or 3 steps away from him. Then —

Without Treats

- Crouch low. Call your pup in a happy voice: "Rover — *Come!*" Keep encouraging him. Hand-claps may help.
- If he comes to you, reward with petting & praise.
- If he doesn't respond, keep calling and *gently* tug him toward you with the leash. *Reel him in*, an inch at a time, if you have to. The important thing is for him to make the connection between the word *"Come"* and the desired response—and enthusiastic *praise* when he reaches you.
- This means you have to praise him whether coming to you was your idea or his.
- Keep repeating until he comes without being tugged.

With Treats

- Call him, as above. When he gets there, reward him with a treat. *Repeat*, but don't use the real treat every time. Pretend you've got one and use the "phantom treat" trick.
- Give treat-rewards at irregular intervals.

With both methods, as your pup starts to get the idea, increase distance to the length of his leash. **Hold the leash** so you can enforce the command. Eventually, he'll start to respond reliably. Then you can try longer distances, using a longer leash or rope so you can still reel him in if you have to.

- You can also start practicing with distractions around you.
- *Only* after he's learned well enough that he comes *every time* you call should you try this off-leash—and even then only inside your

home or a fenced-in yard. If your off-leash pup fails to respond every time, go back to leash-work.

- *Only* after extensive off-leash work in a safely-enclosed space should you even *consider* allowing your dog off-leash in open spaces. It only takes one failure to come when called for a dog to run away, or be hit by a car.

My own dogs are never off-leash outdoors, for a simple reason: I know I haven't worked with them enough to trust them to come every time time I call under uncontrolled conditions. And it's not worth risking my dogs' safety just so they can have a little extra freedom.

- So, *please be very, very careful* about this.
- Your pup should learn to come immediately when called.
- *Never* call your dog to come to you if you're mad, or want to scold him. You don't want him to associate coming when called with negative reinforcement.
- If you need to correct or scold him—or do anything he won't like, such as nail-clipping, ear-drops, etc.—you have to go and get him.

Puppy School - Class 4

"Sit-Stay"

WHY   A *very* important command. Once mastered, it gives you a way to control your pup's behavior, on or off-leash. But he has to know how to *"Sit"* when told before you can add *"Sit-Stay"* to his repertoire. Don't expect miracles. *Encourage* progress. **Be patient & positive.** *"Stay"* can be tricky to teach. Unlike *"Sit,"* it's hard to show your pup the *absence* of activity. In addition, there are three factors that complicate the *"Stay"* command:

- length of time: the longer a pup is asked to stay, the more likely his attention will wander, and so will he
- distance: the farther away you go, the more he'll want to follow you
- distractions: make it tougher for a pup to focus

HOW   First, get your pup's attention & get him to sit.

- Stand facing or alongside him. Swing your flat/open palm (in a "stop" gesture) toward his face & say *"Stay"*
- Don't move. It's OK to repeat the command "Stay" to help him associate the word with staying still. If pup stays for even a few seconds, release him by saying "Okay" and reward with gentle praise. Don't get him too excited.
- Once your pup seems to understand *"Stay,"* gradually increase the length of *"Stay"* time, a few seconds at a time. Don't rush this. Read his body language—try to time your release before he breaks himself from the *"Stay."*
- If he breaks first, correct him with a firm but gentle *"No"* and start over.
- Once he gets the idea, then add some distance. Back away—one step at a time. Don't rush this either. If he continues to stay for a few seconds, move back to him, give gentle praise, and release him with *"okay."*
- Eventually, move back the length of his leash.

As your pup becomes reliable with "Sit-Stay" you can add more distance with the use of a longer leash or a sturdy rope-line tied securely to his collar. Also, start practicing outdoors where he'll be exposed to distractions.

Practice Exercise

Put a treat on the floor a few feet away from your on-leash pup. Ask him to *"Sit-Stay"* and enforce with the leash. When he does it (for increasing lengths of time), release with *"OK"* and let him gobble up the waiting treat.

Puppy School - Class 5

Toys & Chewing

Puppies *need* to chew. Puppies *like* to chew—for a variety of reasons:

- To relieve teething pain
- To relieve stress
- For fun
- Out of boredom

Puppies may be teething on and off until they're 7 or 8 months old. Make sure they have plenty of sturdy chew toys. If you catch your pup chewing on something off-limits (furniture, woodwork, or small items like shoes), *stop bad behavior* by distracting your pup with a "shake can" (an empty soda can with some pennies or hardware inside to produce a loud rattle), a hand-clap, or a stern "*No!*" or "*Leave it!*" Then *correct* your pup and encourage good behavior by giving him a chew toy, and a cheery "*Good dog!*"

- Try home-made chew toys: wet an old washcloth or two. Roll them, or tie into a knot. Then freeze them. When your pup chews on one, the cold helps relieve teething pain. But make sure you retrieve the washcloth-toy before it thaws, or your pup might get the idea that any towel is fair game.

Stores carry a wide variety of toys: Rawhide. Hard Nylabones. Slightly softer Gumabones. Real bones. Plush & rubber toys with squeakers. Almost *all* toys pose *some* hazard to your pup.

- Large *rawhide* chunks may cause digestive blockage when swallowed.
- *Nylabones* and *real bones* may chip or break teeth. Swallowing too many *Gumabone* chunks can cause vomiting.
- *Plush & rubber toys* can be shredded, and your pup may swallow stuffing or choke on the squeakers inside.
- *Rope toys* can be chewed apart; ingested string can get wrapped around intestines and cause *fatal* complications!

So what should you do?

- ❧ Observe your pup at play and **use common sense!**
- ❧ Toys that can be swallowed whole or in large pieces should be played with **only** while you're present.
- ❧ Same with toys containing internal squeakers.

- Dogs love edible toys that were formerly part of an animal (like *rawhide* or *pig's ears*). They like to chew these toys until they're soft enough to tear pieces off and swallow them. To keep your dog safe, monitor the situation: when the toy is nice and soft and slimy, trade it for a fresh one. As it dries, the soft rawhide hardens again. This not only keeps your pup from eating potentially-hazardous chunks, it also makes the toys last longer—and saves you money!

- To lessen the chances of broken teeth, give your pup a varied selection of toys so he doesn't chew only one kind all the time.

- If you don't want your pup chewing on slippers or shoes, *don't* leave them where he can get to them!

- *Don't* give your pup old shoes (or other household items or clothing) to play with. He can't tell the difference between old and new.

NEVER give your dog leftover bones from chicken, turkey, steak-ribs, fish or pork!!

Powerful pup jaws and sharp teeth can break such bones into jagged shards that may cause serious injury when swallowed!

Grown-up dogs need and like to chew, too. So always make sure your pet, no matter what age, has several chew toys at all times. Some experts suggest leaving a half-dozen toys down at any one time. Keep other toys in a box or cabinet. Then, from time to time, "rotate" the toys: pick up "old" ones and put out some "new" ones.

- **No-Chew Stuff**: If your pup starts chewing furniture or woodwork, try using *Bitter Apple*. This venerable product is a harmless but bitter-tasting concoction. (Note on the Puppy Prep Shopping List: Stuff to Buy that there are two types of *Bitter Apple*: liquid and ointment. Use the right one for the job.)

  Liquid *Bitter Apple* evaporates within a few minutes, and the effect wears off. So be prepared to re-spray as needed.

  You can also use various "hot sauces" or even Vicks VapoRub. If your pup chews on his leash, spray *Bitter Apple* on that portion of the leash. Do this repeatedly until he gets discouraged.

"Down"

WHY   Even more than *"Sit,"* teaching a dog *"Down"* gives you an effective way to control unwanted behaviors like jumping up, snatching food off countertops, and begging at the dinner table. *"Down"* is more relaxing than *"Sit"*—so a pup who learns *"Down-Stay"* is less likely to be a pest.

HOW   *"Down"* can be taught with or without treats. Best to practice when your pup is a bit tired, and on a slippery floor (less traction to help him resist).

- Have your pup sit. *Praise* him. Then kneel or crouch in front of or next to him.

- Say *"Down,"* and *gently* slide your pup's front legs forward. You can also press *gently* on his shoulders. Or apply slight downward pressure on his leash. Reward with calm praise, petting and/or a treat. Release by saying *"OK."*

- Phase out your physical "assistance" as your pup learns what *"Down"* means.

— OR —

- Hold treat right in front of pup's nose. As you say *"Down,"* lower the treat to the floor and pull it slightly away from pup. (Have her on a short leash, so she can't grab the treat).

- Reward with praise and a treat. Phase out actual treats. Use "phantom treat" method, with occasional real ones.

Puppy School - Class 6

Teaching "Wait!"

WHY   Teaching your dog *not* to dart out an open door—whether on-leash or off—could save your dog's life. Teaching him not to run into the living room until you've dried his wet, muddy feet could save your carpet.

HOW   Put his leash on. Take him to the door.

- Open the door—but *don't* let him charge ahead. *Stop* him with the leash—and the word *"Wait."* If he pauses, say "Good dog—*wait.*"

- Make him *"Wait"* a few seconds before saying *"OK"* and letting him go. *Don't* let him go until you say *"OK."* If you practice this *every* time you go out a door, your dog can learn to *"Wait"* whenever you say so, whether he's on a leash or off.

Or try this variation:

- Do *"Sit-Stay"* first. Then open the door, say *"Wait,"* and you go out first. Your dog doesn't get to follow until you say *"OK"* (that all-purpose "release" word). If he breaks the stay, he doesn't get to go out.

- *Repeat* until he does what you want. But you have to be fair: don't try this when you know your pup has to go the bathroom *right this instant!*

Giving Pills: "A Spoonful of Sugar..."

In addition to regular heartworm-prevention pills (either daily or monthly), there will be occasions when you'll need to give your pup medication. Most pills should be given with food to lessen the chance of digestive upset. Are their ways to give pills without shoving them down your dog's throat? Yes!

- Try hiding the pill inside a glop of plain yogurt. Or in a glob of cream cheese or peanut butter. Or folded inside a slice of butter. Any of these can be placed on top of your dog's regular meal.

Most dogs are so thrilled to have a special "whipped-cream" treat with their dry food that they gobble it up without ever realizing there's a pill inside. The trick is, the pill must be totally hidden.

Just make sure your dog isn't a sneaky pooch who spits the pill out after he's done eating!

Puppy School - Class 7

Puppy-Proofing Your Home

Did you know your home is *filled* with great stuff to chew on? Your *puppy* knows this. And she can't wait to get to work—on your *furniture*, your *walls*, your *fuzzy slippers*... There's an incredibly simple way to prevent this: *Don't* give pups and young dogs unsupervised free run of your home. And get down on your hands and knees for a dog's-eye view of what looks interesting. Then do the best you can to puppy-proof the place:

- It only takes one wrong bite on an electrical cord to injure or kill your pet. So put power cords out of reach.
- If you can't do that, then keep your pup out of rooms where cord-temptation exists—unless you're there to supervise at all times.
- Never let pups eat house-plants. Many will cause illness.
- Use Bitter Apple to discourage unwanted chewing. (See **Stuff to Buy** on page 151.)

At times when you simply can't supervise your pup, ask him to go into his crate or a puppy-safe room (like your kitchen) closed off with a baby gate. Give him a treat for being a good boy, make sure he's got a few sturdy toys to keep him busy...and *don't* feel guilty!

On-Leash vs. Off-Leash

I've never quite understood why some otherwise sane urban and suburban dog-owners are so determined to let their pets run free. The truth is, few dogs are sufficiently well-trained to be let off-leash in open parks, fields or school-yards—let alone on public streets!

Even if your dog listens to you a spectacular 98% of the time, that still leaves a small but real chance that he'll run across a street to chase a squirrel or greet a dog-pal. And the risk is much greater for puppies—no matter how hard you've worked on *stay*, *wait* and *come*. Puppies are much more likely to give in to impulse and fail to listen at a key moment.

No puppy should ever be let off-leash outdoors unless in a fenced-in, escape-proof area.

- *Leashes are the law* in most suburban and urban locales.
- Leashed dogs are safe.
- *Off-leash dogs* can be hit by cars—ingest poisonous substances—get into fights with other pets—be bitten by wild animals—or even run away.
- Brief freedom to run isn't worth your dog's life, is it?
- Please use *common sense!* Keep your pet *safe & healthy!*

Why Walks Are Good

Dogs *need* walks with us. Letting your dog out in the yard to go to the bathroom *doesn't* substitute for daily walks.
- Walks give you both exercise
- Walks on pavement help keep pup's nails short
- Walks are a bonding experience for you and your dog
- Walks help build your pup's confidence & let him experience the world with you there to protect him and reassure him

Teaching Your Dog to "Heel"

WHY To avoid getting towed down the street by a rambunctious puppy. Or dragging a lazy-bones behind us. In fact, not-so-great leash-walking manners are among the most common complaints to trainers. Teaching your pup to walk with you makes walks fun for both of you. It's worth the effort.

- So why do puppies (or untrained older dogs) pull and lunge? Simple: they want to get from *here* to *there*.
- Sometimes there's actually something special over there they want to reach: a person, another dog, a hero sandwich plopped on the pavement. Sometimes it's just the excitement of exploration—especially for puppies, who seem to want to explore the whole world all at once.
- To get this under control, and actually enjoy walks, we teach our pups to "heel"—to walk close to your left leg, at your pace. He doesn't have to be glued to you. He *does* have to walk without pulling or lagging.

HOW   When you take your pup out, give him a chance to go to the bathroom first. Then, after he goes—or looks like he probably won't go this time out—both of you can focus on heeling. You can try teaching heeling with a regular buckle collar, chain training collar (the common "choke" chain), or the latest and possibly most effective collar: the *Head Halter*. With a head halter, it takes *much* less effort to correct your dog's direction, speed and behavior. It does take some practice for both you and your pup to get accustomed to the different techniques needed with a head halter. But if you're patient, you'll be rewarded. (For more on this, see **Head Halters: New Way to Walk Your Dog** back on page 154.)

Method 1 - Begin with your pup *sitting* at your left.

- As you step out, starting with your left foot (because it's closest to your pup), give the leash a "snap" and say, "Rover, heel!" in a cheerful voice.
- This works better if you walk fairly quickly.
- If your pup lags, encourage him to follow. *Don't* make this a "tug-of-war."
- If your pup pulls ahead, give him a corrective tug on the leash as you say *"No."* Then repeat the command. If he pulls again, repeat the correction.
- Practice changing directions, walking in circles, rounding corners.
- Don't forget—*Praise* him when he's good!

Method 2 - Start as above.

- Set a brisk pace—but remember that speed is relative! Give short dogs a break.
- If your pup pulls, simply *reverse direction* without warning. (To avoid getting dizzy, feel free to go in different directions: zig-zag; triangles, or any shape you choose—the idea is to change direction abruptly).
- If your pup doesn't change with you, he'll *self-correct* when he reaches the end of the leash. Momentum will force him to follow you. *Praise* him when he does.
- Repeat. Soon, most pups think of this as a new *"Which way?"* game. They watch closely to anticipate the next new direction. They start prancing beside you. They're paying attention! And an attentive puppy is more likely to go where you go.
- Every time he changes direction and follows, *Praise* him.

Method 3 - If your pup pulls, simply *stop.*

- Since you outweigh him, and have the element of surprise in your favor, he'll stop too.
- As soon as he halts, *praise* him and continue ahead.
- *Repeat* every time he pulls. You may not get very far—but that's the point. Your dog will soon get the idea that pulling doesn't get him where he wants to go.

Method 4 - If your pup lags behind, or refuses to walk, *don't* drag him!

- Try walking backwards, facing him, and encourage him to follow. Squeak a toy to get his attention.
- You can also try the "cheat" method: carry a tasty treat in the palm of your hand closest to his nose. Let him know it's there. Use it as a "lure" to get him to follow. *Don't* give him the treat until the walk is complete. *Don't* overuse this method, or you may find your smart pup refusing to walk unless you've shown him the treat first.

There's no way to tell which method will work best with your puppy. Try alternating among them. The great thing about teaching your dog to walk properly on a leash is, you don't have to set aside special time to practice. Just incorporate teaching into your daily walks.

Once your pup has gone to the bathroom, practice *"Heel"* for a few minutes during the rest of your walk—every time you walk.

- As he develops good walking "manners," give him some "slack" to wander and sniff. He doesn't have to "heel" all the time.
- Make walks fun, and your dog will have an incentive to learn good leash manners.
- Once your pup has the idea of heeling, start asking him to "Sit" each time you stop. The goal is to make him do an *automatic* sit every time you stop. Reward with praise!

CHOKE-COLLAR WARNINGS

❧ If you use a chain training collar, put it on correctly: with pup on your left, the ring to which you hook the leash *must come over the top* of your dog's neck.

❧ Try to keep the training collar *high* on his neck, just under his ears and chin.

❧ With this type of collar, you'll "snap" the leash with a flick of your hands. Done sharply, this causes the loop to tighten quickly around your dog's neck—but then you MUST release and allow the loop to loosen again. If it fails to loosen, you're using it incorrectly, and your dog *can* choke.

❧ If you jerk the leash too hard, there's a real risk of injuring your dog's neck or throat.

❧ **Choke-chains should *not* be used on small-breed dogs, dogs with flattened muzzles (such as pugs and various Asian breeds) or young puppies.**

❧ A tug on a regular collar is more than enough to make your point. *Please—be careful!*

❧ If you have questions, please consult a trainer or vet.

"Down-Stay"

WHY   As noted earlier, *"Sit-Stay"* is great for establishing some control over your pup's behavior. A dog sitting and staying isn't jumping or pulling. But *"Sit-Stay"* isn't always a relaxing position, especially if your puppy is on a slippery floor. The rear slides, the feet slips, so he eventually stands up to get stabilized.

"Down-Stay" is much more relaxed. Less chance of begging at the table or tackling Grandma as she comes in the front door.

In a dinnertime *"Down-Stay,"* he might even doze off—unless of course a meatball scoots out of your plate and onto the floor. Then he's ready to pounce on the errant morsel before it can escape.

HOW   Teach this *on-leash* first.

- Put your pup in the *"Down"* position.

- Say *"Stay"* as you give the open-palm "stop" hand signal.

- Don't move. If pup stays for even a few seconds, release pup with *"OK"* and *praise*.

- If he breaks first, correct with *firm but gentle "No"* and leash-tug. Start over.

- It's OK to repeat the *"Stay"* command to remind him what he's doing.

- By now (we hope), your pup already understands *"Stay,"* so he should grasp *"Down-Stay"* pretty quickly. Gradually increase the time he stays.

- Then add some distance (back off to end of leash).

- If you're trying this at the dinner table, you can place your foot firmly on the leash 12-18 inches from your pup's neck. If he starts to rise, you'll know it immediately, and you'll keep him from getting up as you repeat the command and praise him once again.

- Eventually, you'll be able to do this without the leash.

Puppy School - Class 8

"Give"

WHY   Puppies can be naturally possessive of toys and food. All pups should be taught to give up anything they have in their mouths. The idea is to accomplish this without getting chomped or wrestling with your pooch. Teach this —
- So your pup understands you're the boss.
- So you can remove anything harmful that he may pick up.
- To make it less likely your dog will bite a child who tries to take a toy away from him.

HOW   Start teaching this as *early as possible!*
- Practice with toys. When your pup has a large chew toy in his mouth, go to him. As you *gently but firmly say "Give,"* grasp the toy. Don't pull it out of his mouth.
- If he gives it up right away, *praise* him! Give him a treat and/or return the toy.
- If he resists or growls, say *"No"* and repeat *"Give."*
- If he continues to resist, *don't* play "Tug-of-War." With one hand, hold him on a short leash, or hold his collar. *Gently* grip his upper lip from above, thumb on one side and forefinger on the other. *Gently* press the lips against the upper teeth. This causes most dogs to open their mouths, or at least loosen their grip. If it works, then take the toy. *Praise* him.
- Try this a few more times. Encourage him to go along. He doesn't have to love this; he does have to accept it.
- Try a similar exercise with food. In mid-meal (with your dog on a leash as a safety measure), simply pick up his dish. If he growls, say *"No."* When he's quiet, *praise* him. Give back the dish. Practice this at odd intervals, so he doesn't expect it. Every time he lets you take his dish, *praise* him and return the dish. But don't tease him.

Rough Play

Don't encourage aggression with roughhousing, wrestling or slap-fighting. It's a good way to get chomped—and if you do, you can't blame your dog.

You have hands—he has teeth—and he'll use them.

If you want to play "Tuggie" with a pull-toy, *you* set the pace and tone. Hold the toy as if you were a tree to which it's attached. Let your dog do all the pulling. And *stop* the game if your pup gets too excited.

Exercise & Play

Dogs of all ages need to exercise and play. It's not enough to let your pup out in a fenced-in yard. He'll probably dig or sleep. Dogs are social animals. Your pup needs to play *with* you. Encourage fetching games with balls and frisbees.

"Settle"

WHY   The *"Settle"* command is a gentle but effective way of getting your pup to *trust* you and recognize your top-dog status. This level of trust means your pup will allow you (and others) to groom him, brush his teeth, or examine any part of his body without struggling, protesting, or biting. (Vet personnel and groomers will *love* you for this!)

HOW   Have your pup lie down on his side or belly while saying something like *"Settle"* or *"Relax."*
- If he struggles, repeat the command and gently enforce it. If he stops struggling, even for a few seconds, praise and pet him. If he starts struggling again, repeat the process.
- Encourage him and teach him he'll be rewarded with belly-rubs & petting. If you make this a pleasant experience, your pup will probably come to enjoy these little sessions.
- Alternate version: kneel on the floor. Get your sitting pup nestled between your knees, facing away from you. Massage and pet him, praise him for relaxing—and sneak a peak at his teeth and ears.

Grooming

Unless they play in the mud, most dogs rarely need baths. They're not supposed to be odorless—although there's a big difference between walking into a room and saying: "Hmm. My dog is here" and "*Ewwww*...my dog is here!"

Too many baths dry out their skin. Instead of frequent baths, groom often with the proper comb or brush for your dog's coat. Use spray deodorants and coat conditioners as you groom to freshen up your pup.

You can get grooming guidance from your vet or a local groomery.

If you do bathe your dog, make sure to use only shampoos formulated for dog skin. And you may want to think about going to one of the new self-service dog-wash places opening in some locales. For a reasonable fee, they have professional washing stations and provide towels and shampoo. And you don't have to clog your own sink or tub with dog hair.

Tooth Care

Doggie teeth are more decay-resistant than ours. (It helps that they don't consume sugar-laden snacks the way humans do.) But they still need care to prevent problems caused by tartar and plaque. Your pup will need periodic cleanings by the vet.

When it's time for a cleaning, don't skip it. It's much less expensive to maintain teeth with preventive care than it is to have emergency dental surgery. Bad tooth hygiene takes a heavy toll on the overall health of many middle-aged dogs—and may shorten their lives by years.

Between cleanings, you can help by brushing your pup's teeth a few times a week. Use only special dog toothpaste, sold by vets and at pet-supply stores. Ask your vet about this. Most dogs aren't thrilled about the brushing, but they love the flavored toothpaste.

Massage

Most dogs love gentle massages. It's a great way to bond with your pup, and it relaxes both of you.

Puppy School - Class 9: Graduation!

"Stay" & Recall

When you first teach "*Stay*," you'll return to your pup's side to praise him and then release him with "*OK*." Why do this instead of calling him to you? Because: this way, he's associating the reward with staying, rather than with coming back to you.

Once he's doing a pretty good "*Stay*," you can start teaching him the recall. Do this by adding the "*Come*" command to either "*Sit-Stay*" or "*Down-Stay*."

Many pups learn the habit of running through everything they know in sequence. Why? Because their owners always train in the same predictable way. Vary your routine. Don't always do "*Sit-Down-Stay-Come*" in order. Mix it up—keep your pup guessing—and he's less likely to get bored. And make sure he actually does what you've asked him to do.

- Practical Application: Sometimes, when you have him "*Stay*," recall him with "*Come*." Other times, you go back to him and reward him for doing a great "*Stay*."

Training With Distractions

Many puppies follow commands well in the quiet and privacy of their own homes or yards. Ideally, your pup should also pay attention in unfamiliar environments. How can you help him accomplish this? By gradually introducing him to distractions, and helping him become desensitized.

- First, practice indoors. Once he understands commands and follows them reliably, have an assistant create distractions by making noise, dropping a heavy book near your dog, jumping, waving arms, etc. Patiently but firmly, remind your pup to pay attention to you and your commands.

- Next, go outside. Work with him in your yard, where new smells and sounds will compete for his attention. Gently and firmly remind him he *must* pay attention to you, and do as you say.

- When he's mastered the yard, work with him on your street, where passing cars and people will distract him. Again, remind him what he's supposed to be doing.

- Don't expect instant miracles. Don't rush the process.

- Gradually, your pup will become used to distractions. With your help, he'll learn to take the big wide world in stride.

Riding in Cars

Safety first! Your pup is safest riding in his plastic travel-style crate.
- This way, he can't move around the car
- He can't interfere with or distract the driver
- He's traveling in his "den"
- He won't go flying if you make a short stop
- In case of accident, he's less likely to panic, get loose, and run into traffic

If your vehicle isn't large enough to fit a crate inside, then check out the variety of doggie travel-harnesses on the market. These fit around your dog's body and interface with standard auto shoulder belts. Used properly, these harnesses can keep your dog from roaming around the interior of your car while you're in motion. They can also keep your pet from flying forward if you make a short stop. Buy one that looks sturdy.

Some dogs develop "travel anxiety." One common reason: the only time they get into a car is to visit the vet. Since many dogs dislike medical exams, this can cause them to become nervous and agitated whenever they're taken to the car. The simplest way to avoid this is to take your pet for rides that end up in fun places.

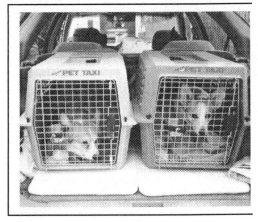

- Go to a park for walks and exercise
- Go to the homes of friends or relatives where your pup gets to enjoy a visit filled with play and petting
- Take him for shopping expeditions to pet-supply places that welcome dogs

Spaying & Neutering

Unless you're planning to breed a purebred puppy with *perfect* temperament and physical characteristics, *please* have your pet neutered. You'll be making sure your dog doesn't bring unwanted puppies into the world. You'll also be protecting your pal's health and you may head off some potential behavior problems *before* they start (especially in male dogs).

- *Female* pups *don't* need to go through a first heat—in fact, you may lose some long-term health benefits of spaying if they do go into heat first.

- *Both* genders should be neutered as early as possible—most vets say at about 5 months of age.

- If your pup hasn't been neutered yet, consult your vet today and find out the right time to do this.

Teaching Fun Doggie Tricks

WHY   Dogs are capable of learning an amazing number of words, phrases and commands. The more you teach your pup, the less likely she is to get bored and develop destructive habits. A busy dog is a happy dog!

So, in addition to basic commands, try teaching your dog some additional "showstopper" tricks.

HOW   The method is the same as in teaching commands.
- Figure out what you want her to do

- Pick a brief command and use consistently

- Show your pup what you want her to do while repeating the command to help her associate the word with the action

- Praise her when she does the trick—even if she only did it because you helped her

- Repeat the process for such tricks as *Shake Hands*, *Roll Over*, *Play Dead*, *"Beg,"* *Take-a-Bow*, and *Fetch*.

Many of these tricks use behaviors your pup does naturally anyway. If you see her doing something that you want to turn into a trick, be alert! For instance, if you see her in a "play-bow" posture, immediately say the phrase *"Take a Bow"* (the single word "bow" sounds too much like "down") and praise her. Do this every time you see her bowing on her own. At first she won't understand. But there's a good chance she'll learn to associate the command with the bow. And then you've got a "circus star"!

There are some excellent books available that deal specifically with teaching tricks. Next time you're at the local bookstore, pick one up. You'll get step-by-step instruction on how to teach all kinds of neat tricks.

Remember to use the same positive-reinforcement techniques as in teaching other basic commands. You and your dog will have a lots of fun. And—David Letterman's famous "Stupid Pet Tricks" notwithstanding—you and your dog will have a great time showing off for friends and family.

That's it. Good luck with your puppy! Please don't forget that having a dog is supposed to be fun! And now for the final lesson I learned from my amazing Mail Order Annie:

Annie taught me...

Teach your puppy well —
with love and respect —
and she'll fill your life with joy
every day you're together!

The End!

(But don't forget to check the books & web sites on the next page...)

Places to Look for More Information

🐾 BOOKS

Dogs Behaving Badly - by Dr. Nicholas Dodman
The Dog Who Loved Too Much - by Dr. Nicholas Dodman
The Intelligence of Dogs - by Stanley Coren
How to Teach Your Old Dog New Tricks - by Ted Baer
The Roger Caras Dog Book - by Roger Caras
The Doctors Book of Home Remedies for Dogs & Cats -
   by the Editors of *PREVENTION* Magazine
UC/Davis School of Veterinary Medicine Book of Dogs -
   edited by Mordecai Siegel
Second-Hand Dog - by Carol Lea Benjamin
Pack of Two - by Caroline Knapp
With Alex by My Side - by Joel Davis

🐾 INTERNET WEB SITES

www.akc.org - American Kennel Club - info and links
www.dog-play.com - Great site with info and lots of links:
   hundreds of creative ways to have fun with your dog
www.avma.org - American Veterinary Medical Association
www.puppyplace.com - Purina site - useful info and links
www.healthypet.com - American Animal Hospital Association
www.petshealth.com - Dr. David Tayman's web site (my vet and
   one of Maryland's best!) - links and info
www.dogfancy.com - major magazine and lots of links
www.pembrokecorgi.org - Pembroke Welsh Corgi Club of
   America
www.delanet.com/~terenelf/ - Pembroke Corgi breeder Lois
   Kay
www.dogtoys.com - lots of toys (featuring the Tricky Treats ball,
   among the best food-dispensing toys ever!)
www.valleyvet.com - pet-product catalog (with free shipping on
   orders over $50)
www.rcsteele.com - pet-product catalog (carries the *Gentle
   Leader*)
www.JemarPet.com - pet-product catalog, a small company
   with a reputation for service

About the Author

Starting with his first Welsh Corgi—the amazing Mail Order Annie—Canine Behavioral Consultant Howard Weinstein has been learning about and teaching puppies and dogs since 1981.

He is now the proprietor of *Day-One Dog Training* in Howard County, Maryland. *Day-One Dog Training* offers both group classes and private at-home sessions. He also presented *Puppy Prep 101* through Howard Community College Continuing Education.

He is also an award-winning writer. This is his twelfth book, including three national and *New York Times* best-sellers.

As a journalist, Howard's articles and columns have appeared in a variety of national publications, including *The New York Times*, *Newsday*, and *Starlog Magazine*.

In the highly competitive New York advertising world, he has won awards from the American Advertising Federation & the Community Agencies Public Relations Association (CAPRA) for writing and producing American Diabetes Association radio public-service campaigns.

In addition to educating pups and their people, Howard has also taught writing classes and workshops at colleges, schools, libraries and conventions for over twenty years.

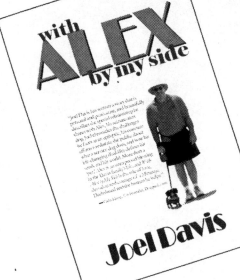